THE BELGIANS

KOEN MATTHIJS
MICHEL DRAGUET

PHOTOGRAPHY BY

Christine Bastin

Herman Bertiau

Lieve Blancquaert

Elisabeth Broekaert

Jacques Evrard

Leopold Oosterlynck

Philip Vanoutrive

Joost Vyncke

THE BELGIANS

The publishers would like to thank the Ministry of Foreign Affairs, Foreign Trade and Development Cooperation, the Belgian Office for Foreign Trade, Inbel, the Belgian Fuji Agency N.V., American Color Lab, and the many institutes, companies and individuals who have contributed in any way to the conception and production of this book.

This book is published simultaneously in 5 languages:
The Belgians,
De Belgen,
Les Belges,
Die Belgier,
Los Belgas.

© Uitgeverij Lannoo nv, Tielt, Belgium.
Coordination:
Uitgeverij Lannoo nv, Tielt and Vandekerckhove & Co, Ghent.
Graphic design:
Vandekerckhove & Co, Ghent.
Typesetting by Vandekerckhove & Co and New Graphic Center
Printed and bound by Drukkerij Lannoo nv, Tielt.
Printed in Belgium - 1993.
2nd revised edition
ISBN 90 209 2291 2 (paperback)
ISBN 90 209 2096 0 (case bound)
D /1993 /45 /142

CONTENTS

"The example of my brother and Queen Fabiola will be a rich source of inspiration for Queen Paola and myself. The values which they so strikingly embodied will guide us in the execution of our duties...

You have just completed the state reform which has transformed Belgium into a federal state; I now look to you to bring these new institutions to life and ensure that they function optimally, in a spirit of solidarity and good will, tolerance and federal good citizenship.

Disturbing manifestations of collective egoism can be observed almost everywhere in the world today; let us demonstrate that men and women who belong to different cultures can live together in harmony in the same country.

Let us practise federal good citizenship, in the knowledge that by doing so, we shall be setting an example for the rest of Europe."

Extract from King Albert II's speech at the swearing-in ceremony on 9 August 1993.

The Kingdom of Belgium (30 518 km²) enjoys a unique geographical location. In the centre of the "Golden Triangle" of Western Europe, ten million people live and work in a land bounded on one side by the grey sandy beaches and dunes of the North Sea (the coastline stretches for 67 kilometres) and on the other by the richly forested hillsides of the Ardennes. This represents a population density of 326 inhabitants per km²: a very high demographic concentration (only the Netherlands is more densely populated) which leaves its mark on the landscape.

In the northern part of the country live almost 5.8 million Dutch-speaking Flemings. South of the capital, Brussels (which is a bilingual island of 1 million inhabitants in the middle of the territory of the Flemish Community), lies Wallonia with its 3.2 million French-speaking inhabitants. In the east there are 60 000 German-speaking Belgians. Between Flanders and Wallonia runs the fifteen-hundred-year-old linguistic and cultural border which has remained almost unchanged over the years, as the interface between the Germanic and the Latin worlds.

The Belgians are a microcosm of the people of Europe.

Belgians are deeply aware of their past history - every day of their lives they see it around them, and carry it with them. It is more than a mere visual awareness of the charming countryside of their land with its historical cities, cathedrals, belfries and narrow medieval streets. Nothing of what Belgium is today - a little corner of Europe which is one of the ten most prosperous countries in the world, where an incredible variety of people and ideas pass through - none of this can be explained without understanding the past, the roots of the people and the painful development of the three languages, cultures and social and political temperaments which grew up on Belgian soil.

Belgium is not particularly rich in natural resources. It is the Belgian people themselves, with their dynamism and will to work, their language skills and inventiveness, who together with Luxembourg, their partners in the Belgium-Luxembourg Economic Union (BLEU), have made their country the ninth greatest trading nation, with the highest exports per capital in the world.

These statistics will give a concrete picture of how the three peoples which make up our nation live and work, and earn our country the reputation of a place where the living is good.

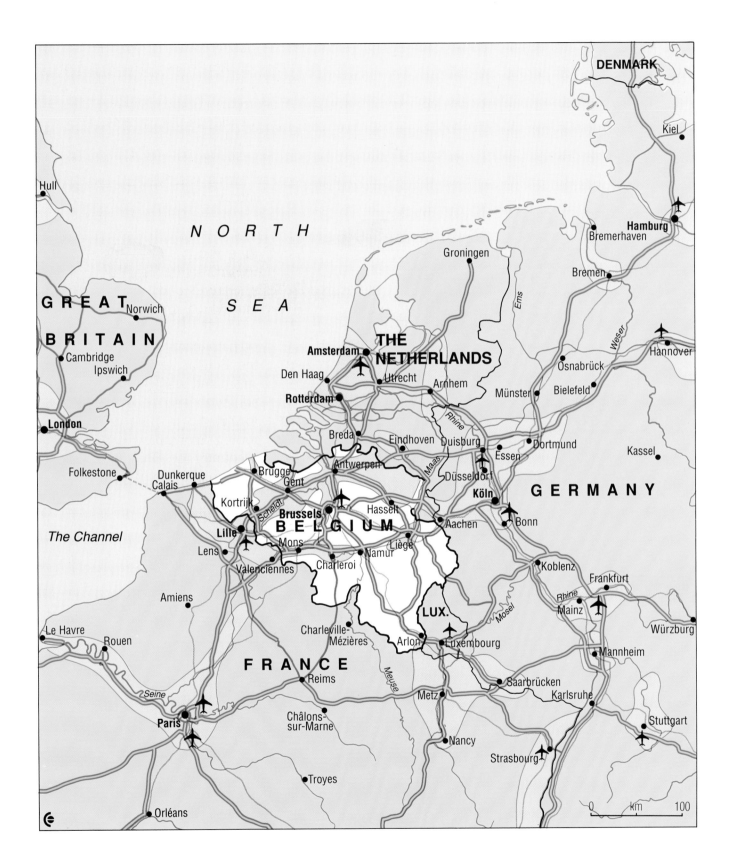

CHAPTER

1

HISTORY & TRADITIONS

*Festival of the
Giants in Ath*

HISTORY & TRADITIONS

*Seeing a country's past
through the eyes of its
inhabitants transforms
our reading of its history.*

The linear progress of time gives way to a subjective interpretation which actively mixes memory and the unconscious, in which everyone draws from the past the elements he needs in order to express his own identity.

In order to understand the essence of a country, we must interrogate what it was in the past in order to discover the particular features which condition its future. Belgium, at the end of our 20th century, is committed to a path of federalism which guarantees the respect of every person within the diversity of cultures on which the country is founded. At the time as the difficult assimilation of Central and Eastern European countries into the orbit of the Europe of the Twelve is posed in terms of resurgent nationalism, Belgium becomes in this way a model of cooperation between communities with differing cultures. Today, Belgians, lacking a national future, have assimilated their destiny to that of Europe. This expansion of horizons corresponds closely to the lessons of our past, which made the area between the Meuse and the Scheldt into a crossroads open to the whole world.

Going back in time, we can ask what makes up Belgium's particular identity. It is not just belgitude, the sense of Belgian specificity. At the turn of the century, the sense of belonging to a nation was based more on sentiment than on reason. For many, the fact of being Belgian revives the memory of past sacrifices. In a country born in the 19th century, the two wars which shook the world apart in 1914-1918 and 1940-1945 welded together in adversity those who were opposed to barbarism and the rule of darkness. National unity was born in war and became incarnated in a spirit of resistance to which Belgians have always remained attached. The image of Albert I, the "Knight King", remains alive in the collective memory, symbolising the resistance and determination of a

Antwerp

people and a state. But Belgium is a country of paradox: just when national unity was becoming more important than class interests, Belgium began a long community identity crisis which twenty centuries of occupation had never succeeded in crystallizing. After 1918, whilst giving to the world the image of a strongly unified country, Flanders and Wallonia were giving different interpretations to a common past and moving towards an antagonism which was to

replace what till then had been only collaboration and understanding. The time of division and secession had come.

The north of the country, essentially rural, was attached to the memory of its soil, whilst the south, faced with uncontrolled industrialization, saw the key issue for the country lying in the combat for democracy. History took on different colours which have remained vivid until today.

*Monument to the
Unknown Soldier
in Brussels*

WHAT IS BELGIUM TODAY

*Belgium is a child of
the 19th century. Born of a revolution
inspired by the Romantic period.*

The birth itself occurred during an opera performance (La Muette de Portici) at the Monnaie opera house. Belgium became a political invention nourished by cultural design. This fact in itself is revealing. The example of the July days pushed the Brussels bourgeois class to claim an independence, which already brought to the surface the differences in sensitivity between North and South. Until 1898, French remained the one official language of Belgium. The 1830 Revolution was represented to the world as the reaction of a French-speaking Catholic bourgeoisie hostile to the Protestant aristocracy of the Orange-Nassau family imposed by the allies in 1815. In cultural terms, Belgium was born of the economic desires of the French-speaking elite which was already leading the country down the path of massive industrialization. The Belgian identity which took shape in 1830 demonstrates a consensus-style pragmatism, accepting the political and strategic compromises imposed from abroad in order to achieve its economic and cultural plans.

Belgium, a new piece on the European chessboard, had to defend its frontiers. In October 1831, the Netherlands violated its integrity, annexing Maastricht, Limburg and German-speaking Luxembourg. The split between the North (Netherlands) and the South (Belgium), born on the barricades of 15 August 1830, consecrated the independence of the new country, soon to have its own constitution (promulgated on 11 February 1831) and monarchy (Saxe-Coburg-Gotha). The constitution set out to unite Enlightenment ideas of progress and traditional political concepts. As such it confirmed the sovereignty of the Nation defended by a constitutional and hereditary monarchy. The image of consensus was solidly established. The choice of sovereign demonstrated a typical spirit of reconciliation and sense of compromise raised to a diplomatic art. The person of Leopold of Saxe-Coburg-Gotha combined the interests of every major power of his time without directly representing any one of them. From 1830 onwards, the monarchy imposed itself as the

*The Provisional
Government -
1830*

primary symbol of national unity. Its birth was achieved in return for the limitation of its foreign ambitions: the European powers meeting in London imposed a perpetual neutrality on the nascent Belgian state.

This notion is not uninteresting. It consecrates the vision of a Belgium which, like a keystone at the centre of Europe, maintains the balance of nations. The newly constituted state of Belgium is acceptable only if it looks in on itself, its right to exist given in return for a renunciation of international ambitions. Here we already have the image of a country which will associate its identity with its own negation. The birth of the Belgian State owes as much to Britain's desire to isolate France as to the incapacity of the Netherlands to weld back together what had been torn apart by the Reformation. Belgium is an artificial country. A central part of its identity is that it tolerates neither strong central power, nor autocratic unitarianism.

The living force of Belgium resides in the strength of its cities, solidly anchored in prosperous and dynamic regions. Seen from a distance, its frontiers appear to be drawn from the outside rather than the inside. The history of 1830 does not belong to the same order of values as that of previous centuries. From Independence onwards, a conflict exists between the logique de l'Etat and the will of the people. For all its historical richness, pre-1830 Belgium exists for its inhabitants only in the form of clichés, symbols, images nourished by a way of life and a tradition of thought. In July 1831 the break was experienced as a country freeing itself from the murderous history of major European powers. From the Burgundians to the Dutch occupation, with Austrian, Spanish and

French overlords along the way, Belgium - a flamboyant anachronism - consisted of a few tracts of land spread out between the North Sea and the Meuse. Having acquired its independence, Belgium was able to satisfy its ambitions: economic development and industrial expansion hand in hand with an intellectual climate dominated by the myth of progress.

Thus the 19th century was to "organize" the Belgian collective unconscious by imposing the image of an independent state, albeit subject to the caprices of its warmongering neighbours and its duty of perpetual neutrality. Belgium was allowed to exist only for itself. Which explains an unpretentiousness and a quality of life which remain very particular to it. And a dynamism which makes it for ever press forwards. In 1835, it was in Belgium that the first railway line on the continent was built. Belgium was viewed as a model of liberalism, a haven for all exiles from less open regimes. Its industrialization was seen as a pillar of progress... Five key economic centres grew up: Ghent, Antwerp, Brussels, the Liège basin and the Mons-Charleroi region. If Flanders was to remain attached to its economic traditions, Wallonia in the first half of the 19th century experienced the mechanization of its heavy industry. This economic development took on a different social significance in the North and South of the country. In Wallonia, high population density and industrial concentration were to favour the development of a sub-proletariat which was to weigh heavily on the political development of the country at the end of the century. The exploitation of the lowest social classes was to permit the concentration of economic and banking empires in Brussels.

Leopold I

At the heart of Europe, Belgium was seen as a country of democracy. Its refusal of any authoritarian centralism distinguished it from France. The newly-constituted Belgium immediately granted substantial autonomy to its local authorities. Like a reminder of its past and of the grandeur of its cities, Belgium's constitution aims to arbitrate in a dialogue between the actors of public life rather than act as the agent of a strong central power.

From the start, Belgium has had a dominant bourgeoisie with, for several decades, a French-speaking culture. In both Antwerp and Ghent, intellectual circles spoke French as the distinctive sign of belonging to an elite. To this cultural domination was to be added, throughout the 19th century, the economic control of a prosperous Wallonia in a process of major industrial expansion. The coal mines of the Borinage, Charleroi and the Liège basin favoured the development of industrial empires as yet unknown in Flanders. If the North of the country was to perceive the constitution of the State as a despoilment, the South was soon to associate it with a capitalist plan foreign to the interests of Wallonia's proletarianized populations. The century was marked by political demands which, both in the North and the South, reflected different and later divergent concerns: a Flemish identity to be restored in the North, the desired triumph of a workers' state in the South were to impose different political developments. Between the two, Brussels became the target of strong criticism. Little by little, Wallonia and Brussels were to move further and further apart in the collective unconscious, setting an impoverished Wallonia against a rich and haughty capital. Where Flanders saw in Brussels part of its territory occupied by French-speakers, Walloons were to equate the capital with the uncontrolled industrialization which

was oppressing them.

The Flemish question, essentially cultural in nature, is mirrored by a Walloon question based on economic crisis and severe social deprivation. Whilst Flanders aspired to the recognition of its traditions and specificity within a dominantly French-speaking Belgium, Wallonia demanded the thoroughgoing transformation of the social order. The economic crisis of its traditional industries, accelerated by the oil crises, was to produce a major upheaval in the social order. The coal mines were closing their gates. Flanders, anxious to affirm itself, was exploiting its new industrial prospects whilst Wallonia was growing poorer. By the end of the sixties, the social and economic relationship between the two had reversed.

Belgium tears itself apart internally, whilst the dramatic moments of history strengthen the sense of cohesion in the collective imagination. Nonetheless, cultural differences, confessional divergencies and political antagonism return every time a crisis is over. The two world wars marking the 20th century were to force destiny by disturbing the economic and social order: 1918 was to impose universal suffrage, 1945 marked the end of the unitarian dream.

If Belgium quarrels, it also knows how to make up. The "Belgian compromise" which has become part of the country's political culture as well as clichés imposed from abroad are part of Belgium's identity, an identity which found its historic expression in the colonial saga born of the Congo inheritance (1908), in the resistance of the Belgian army on the river IJzer in 1914, and in its defiant opposition to the Nazi invader in 1940. The symbol of this unity throughout these testing times, the Royal Dynasty has formed the cement of a common will expressed independently of individuals' regional attachments. Belgium's identity affirms itself as an an-

Le Grand Hornu

swer to history, a defensive reflex when danger threatens. Is it not therefore logical that this sentiment will change in the wake of the new reality imposed by the Europe of the regions promised for 1993 ?

In 1970-1971 the Constitution recognized four linguistic Regions: Flanders, Wallonia, the German-speaking cantons and Brussels. The status of Brussels was to pose a problem until 1989, when it elected its Regional Council and formed its first Executive. The Regions and Communities were officially constituted as far back as 1970. Ten years later, they were given Executives separate from the central power.

The institutional development of the country has been towards a federalism which guarantees the specificity of each of the parties. Within this context, the history of each of the Communities contributes to defining its deep identity and, undoubtedly, to developing new forms of collaboration between Communities in which unity would be born of diversity. History, coloured with folklore, tradition and a high quality art de vivre remains the best visiting card of this entente pacifique.

Does today's Belgium seek to efface the memory of 1830 by substituting a double reality which is both broader and more intimate ? A European ambition which would erase its frontiers, leaving it with the reality of its cities and regions ? Belgium's future lies in this a typical destiny which finds its unity in the respect of its diversity, and is founded on the extension of our country's horizons to the European level.

We must look deeper. What role will history play for this country whose institutional physiognomy is in a state of perpetual change ?

We must point out from the beginning that the State is viewed by Belgians as something opaque and nebulous. The State, the Communities, the Regions, their pertinence and limits, are all jumbled up in the collective unconsciousness. The institutions are made doubly complex by their lack of symmetry. Wallonia and Brussels live in two distinct economic regions which nonetheless combine forces in "personalized" matters (education, health, culture etc.) within a larger entity called the French-speaking Community. In the north of the country, the Flemish Community constitutes a vast entity in charge of both personalized and economic matters. The powers of each Community are not determined solely by geography. Brussels, the majority of whose inhabitants are French-speaking, and which has enjoyed increasingly real independence since 1989, is the subject of the attentions of both communities. To the east, the German-speaking Community, with its own Executive, lives in a close relationship with the Walloon Region.

Is Belgium destined to disappear ? The question is a genuine one. Nonetheless it seems certain that the independence of the Communities will provide the basis for effective collaboration around values which continue to be held in common. Belgium's identity is no abstraction. It is no doubt expressed less within our frontiers than by the image which the world has developed of this "in-between" country. Belgium's identity remains half-way between its history and its art de vivre. A certain savour no doubt felt more strongly by foreigners than by Belgians themselves, who are too close to their own roots and past. Belgium is born of time, but time has largely contributed to untying what has held it together.

Colonial monument in Ostend

HISTORY & TRADITIONS

This federalist development did not happen by chance. This loss of power by the central State has been balanced by increased powers for local authorities (provinces, communes), grouped within Communities and Regions, thus favouring the identification of their populations with their own institutions. These transformations

lead to a search for the roots and traditions within which each Community will find its own reference system. As frontiers become blurred, looking back through the generations to the past enables us to grasp a tradition which guarantees the future.

Memorial of the Battle of Bastogne, 1944

THE PAST AS A PROMISE FOR THE FUTURE

Until 1830, the history of what was to become Belgium appears marked by a series of upheavals which for a long time prevented identification with a State.

The people of Belgium never succeeded in uniting into a nation, with an image with which it could identify. As far back as the Gallic Wars (1st century B.C.), this unity was missing. Caesar describes the small nations between the North Sea and the Meuse as being in constant dispute. Since the Roman domination the "Belgian area" appears vowed to division and separation. Indeed, whilst the southern part was genuinely marked by Latin culture, the northern tribes escaped Romanization more or less entirely.

Ypres

Belgian unity already appears as good as impossible, even if the middle of the 5th century sees the whole area under the single law of the Frankish Kingdom.

Within this dissonant geography, certain cities grew in importance. Tongeren, the ancient capital of the Eburones, became a bishopric in around 343; a century later, Clovis established his capital at Tournai. Around these cities, regions began to organize themselves. The development of means of communications rendered them rapidly prosperous (from the 8th century, the Rhine-Meuse axis was to play its part in the growth of the valley of the Meuse). From the outset, the "Belgian area" was defined as a key European crossroads.

The regions between the Meuse and the Scheldt, an area of dialogue, have also formed a buffer between the major powers which have attempted to organize themselves over the course of history. Each time the Empire was divided up, our regions became the subject of strife. From the Treaty of Verdun (843) to the break-up of the Napoleonic Empire (1814-1815), frontiers inevitably passed through Belgium. Tossed by the hazards of history, the "Belgian area" would for a short time dream of developing into a huge empire of the centre. A vain dream, for narrow Lotharingia, born of the break-up of Charlemagne's empire at Verdun, did not long withstand the appetites of its neighbours. Deprived of Flanders, offered to what would one day be France, it was attached from 925 onwards to the German territories of Louis the German. The Scheldt became the dividing line between France and Germany and the area of what was to become Belgium discovered its vocation as a battlefield.

Deprived of a national - or nationalist - destiny, our regions still aspired to the independence which the ephemeral Lotharingia had given it for a moment. Liège, Brabant and Hainaut conquered an autonomy which, on the other side of the frontier, Flanders, by then a county, also wrested from its French suzerains.

These regions based their independence on their prosperity. Taking advantage of their good climate and their location at the crossroads of the largest navigable waterways in Western Europe, they became obvious focal points of development. The land was fertile and its trade routes allowed traders to penetrate deep into the continent. The organization of labour al-lowed large cities to grow up equalled only by those of Northern Italy. Contacts developed, with their particular cultural expression: the humanist image of the Italian Renaissance is matched by the Christian intimacy of the Flemish Primitives (Van Eyck, Van der Weyden, Memling etc.) and the symbolic quality of prestigious craftsmanship (Brabant altarpieces and the work of Liège goldsmiths). This sense of identity was not national, but regional. It was especially strong in Liège where, since 980, prince-bishops exercised temporal power over the principality. This awareness was attached not only to the image of a dynasty but also to the symbols of its political and financial institutions. People identified themselves with the symbols of their cities - their belfries and 'perrons' - preferring the extended powers of municipalities and wealthy bourgeoisies to the despotism of monarchs. From the 12th century onwards, the cities won their freedom. Bruges developed prodigiously to become one of Europe's leading cities. The ideal of these cities heralds that of 1789: cities are ruled with a sense of morality and discipline, of rights and duties, as well as an emphasis on protecting the individual who is required to participate in the life of the State.

These regions looked forward to power being vested in cities and their regions, without giving rise to a centralized and authoritarian state. Even if Belgium did not then exist, a sense of complementarity nonetheless grew up between the cities: metalworking in the principality of Liège, textiles in Flanders and Brabant, agriculture in Luxembourg and Hainaut. The "Belgian area" was becoming more interested in trading - and its relationship with England - than the games being played on the political chessboard. The Hundred Years War was to ravage the countryside and submit the cities to the fury of French and English troops. The Battle of the

Tournai

Golden Spurs (1302) and the pro-English uprising in Ghent led by Jacques Van Artevelde in the midst of the Hundred Years War left fewer marks on history than on Flemish consciousness which later saw in them the symbol of a Flemish identity oppressed by a French-speaking elite. The collective subconscious drew from it the necessary emotional charge to awaken a consciousness of Flemish identity.

Economic advance and political power found their unique expression when Philip the Bold, Duke of Burgundy, added Flanders and Artois to his possessions. This marked the beginning of a bitter struggle between France and Burgundy, the victor of which was to build a great modern state on the ruins of its enemy. The balance of power in Europe was once again called into question. The Burgundian dream replaced that of Lotharingia, creating a state between France and Germania at the heart of Europe. The interests of the States found themselves opposed to those of the cities. At the same time as its merchants spread Bruges' name and renown far over the seas, war ravaged the countryside and Liège was exposed repeatedly to the fury of the Burgundians. From these troubled times the collective memory would later recall the spirit of resistance of the 600 men of Franchimont and the desolation of Liège devastated in 1468 by Charles the Bold. It would also retain the memory of the freedom of its cities and the prosperity of its regions.

The hopes of the House of Burgundy were blotted out in 1477 in the snows of Nancy. Charles the Bold disappeared from the scene offering his daughter Mary and his lands to the Habsburg family. Our regions, now known as the Netherlands, passed to Maximilian of Austria, soon to be consecrated Emperor. Our unity was born out of absorption. Firstly by Austria, then by Spain, with the *Liège* marriage in 1496 of Philip I to

Jeanne, daughter of the Reyes Catolicos of Spain. This abstract game of inheritances no doubt distanced the populations from their suzerains. Popular identity was to be forged by day-to-day life rather than on the parchment of treaties and successions. As the Netherlands passed from Austrian to Spanish rule, the cities grew and became more powerful through trade and crafts. Parallel with the gradual constitution of the major modern states of Europe, our regions grew up around their cities. Two antagonistic conceptions of the future began to take shape: raison d'Etat and the pragmatism of the free cities.

Despite the brilliant memories left by Charles V's reign (the constitution of the "Circle of Burgundy" in 1548, with Brussels as its capital), the leading citizens were soon forced to bow to the orders of his successor, Philip II. The Netherlands, integrated into a single powerful unit with an effective administration, reacted to what was perceived as Spanish occupation. The Germanic Holy Roman Empire reigned over an undivided Europe, from whose shores it set sail to conquer the world, without realizing that, within its borders, a sense of identity was growing up opposed to the autocratic rule of Philip II.

The grandeur of states is frequently the cause of their decline. The prudent Spaniards organized their empire, placing Margarita of Parma at the head of the Netherlands. The Reformation, distilling virulent criticism of the Church, threatened the equilibrium of the State. Philip II did not hesitate to send north the disturbing figure of the Duke of Alba, backed by the Holy Inquisition. Our regions, with their traditional tolerance, were to discover the cruelty of a church at the service of a raison d'Etat. In 1576, after the Spanish fury had borne down on Antwerp, the frontier was drawn between a northern and southern Netherlands at the Pacification of Ghent (1576).

The former Netherlands fell apart. To the North, the Protestants put up a ferocious resistance to the Spaniards, creating an independent state based on the "Union of Utrecht" (1579). To the South, the Catholics organized themselves, achieving a sort of semi-independence under the tutelage of their Governor-General. The image of national unity was possibly born during this feverish period, symbolized by the brilliant reign of Archdukes Albert and Isabella (1598-1621).

Between the United Provinces and the Netherlands, a frontier grew up defined less by geography and more by religious confession. Between 1635 and 1648, the Dutchmen from the United Provinces prosecuted a relentless war against the Southern Netherlands, wresting from it Flemish Zeeland and Northern Brabant. Within this vast whole, the Principality of Liège took advantage of its autonomy to develop and constitute a powerful enclave within the Spanish territories.

Spain's grasp weakened and its northern possessions became fragile just as Louis XIV's France was searching to find its natural frontiers. The ancient Burgundian dream became a French reality when Artois (1659), part of Flanders (1667-1668 and 1672-1678) and Hainaut (1672-1678) passed under the French crown.

In 1713, as a result of the Treaty of Utrecht, designed to establish a new European order following the War of the Spanish Succession, the Netherlands returned to Habsburg Austria. Once again, this country passed peaceably through the major changes in history without being able to decide its own destiny. The Spanish parenthesis came to an end, leaving our cities with a number of painful memories and the splendour of a Baroque culture.

The Austrian domination was to coincide with the economic growth of the Southern Netherlands, even if the Austrians at first maintained the autocratic character of the Spanish occupation. Our country was one of the most populated of Europe, with a rising prosperity and industrialization which were to mark Wallonia to the core. Mines were opened up, the glass industry flourished and metalworking grew in importance. The Church was influenced by the Enlightenment, which also guided the enlightened sovereigns. A new division was taking place within our area. Wallonia was moving away from the Catholic North, allying with the philosophers in its desire for independence. The role of the Church was called into question, and education began to be organized.

The French Revolution imported into our country the ideal of a modern lay State. The Brabançon rising of 1789 failed to remove the Austrians and our territory became a battlefield once again. The coalition against the French Republic was beaten firstly at Jemappes (1792) and then at Fleurus (1794). The Republic was now safe to organize its new possessions, which included the Netherlands, the principality of Liège and the territory abandoned by Holland. In 1795, pre-Reformation Netherlands was reconstituted in the form of 9 departments under French rule. The bourgeoisie of the cities took advantage of this new power to continue the industrialization of our regions: textiles in Flanders, coal in Wallonia, metalworking in the Liège area became major industrial poles.

Our regions, absorbed into what was soon to be the Napoleonic Empire, threw themselves into the epic without flinching from sacrifice. They were to leave them exhausted. A split had developed which the defeat at Waterloo in 1815 was to intensify. The French annexation had favoured a bourgeois ideal nourished by the

Bruges

spirit of the Enlightenment, separating the Flemish people from the French-speaking élite. At Waterloo, the French Army included large numbers of Walloons, whilst the coalition armies rallied Dutch and Flemish troops under their flags. For the first time, diverging interests and opinions took the form of organized confrontation.

After this slaughter, our regions passed under Dutch rule as part of the United Kingdom of the Netherlands. Whilst the Netherlands recovered their former territorial unity, mentalities had changed and differences had become rooted. The heavy-handedness of the House of Orange-Nassau further fuelled the rancour. Dutch-speaking Protestants in the North and French-speaking Catholics in the South were no longer able to live within the same boundaries. Revolutionary ideas, a permanent feature of the South, were soon to flare up again. Belgium would be born of this divergence of interests and intentions.

The Lion of
Waterloo

*Flower carpet
with St Michael,
the patron saint of
Brussels*

HISTORY AND BELGIAN IDENTITY

Our intention has not been simply to retrace the history of this young country in its present form, but to attempt to grasp, via this past, the way in which Belgians understand their country.

History bears witness to the slow growth to maturity of a consciousness. It is important to trace the profile of this consciousness. Belgians give, first and foremost, the image of a national consciousness attached to a landscape - the North Sea with its greys and ochres, or the dense forests of the Ardennes - and to a certain way of life. Belgians remain unconcerned by the destiny of nations. A Belgian is more attached to his region, to the city which gives it its heartbeat, and to the countryside which gives it its colours. When describing his country, the Belgian

The North Sea beach in Blankenberge

will define it in negative terms, talking of the Country where you never arrive (Pierre Mertens), drawing a picture of what Belgium is not as in Luc de Heusch's This is not Belgium or boasting, with a disillusioned pride, of the Grief of the Belgians (Hugo Claus).

What is essentially Belgian may well be this ability to affirm oneself by a summation of frustrations. In Belgium, tolerance takes this strange form of self-derision. Belgium's historic memory closely conditions its culture. This mechanism, in itself, has a symbolic value. It projects

Belgium's historic destiny onto human beings: a country of "irregulars" which finds its shape only with the movement of the larger states enclosing it. Belgium's fate has never been the primary concern, it is settled in the final lines  of a Treaty, providing the keystone of a continuously changing balance, the final piece of a jigsaw puzzle·which imposes on it its perpetual neutrality and its European destiny. A country of memories which has long time dreamt of an Empire of the Centre, a country of traditions, culture and craftsmanship, devoid of nationalist dreams and chauvinist ambitions; a country of the via media, a historic mirage which, scarcely formed, began to disintegrate... like those sand castles which Flemish and Walloon children build between the sky and the sea to scan the horizon for a destiny which exchanges the weight of statehood for the adventure of a Europe of the regions.

CHAPTER

2

A PROFILE
OF THE PEOPLE

THE BELGIANS

THE POPULATION OF BELGIUM

In 1830, at the dawn of the Belgian state, the population numbered 3.8 million.

AVERAGE ANNUAL POPULATION GROWTH AND SIZE OF POPULATION IN THE LAST YEAR OF EACH PERIOD (1831-1991)					
	Flanders	Wallonia	Brussels	Belgium	Total population (in last year)
1831-1846	12 970	17 034	4 457	34 461	4 337 196
1847-1856	486	13 828	4 912	19 226	4 529 460
1857-1866	8 982	15 999	4 857	29 837	4 827 833
1867-1880	20 215	20 126	9 099	49 441	5 520 009
1881-1890	27 871	18 715	8 345	54 931	6 069 321
1891-1900	32 046	19 785	10 591	62 423	6 693 548
1901-1910	39 745	19 698	13 580	73 024	7 423 784
1911-1920	940	-7 219	4 457	-1 822	7 465 782
1921-1930	40 691	12 936	8 573	62 201	8 092 004
1931-1947	24 338	-3 370	3 750	24 717	8 512 195
1948-1961	36 573	7 045	4 776	48 396	9 189 741
1962-1970	39 179	6 250	5 816	51 245	9 650 944
1971-1980	21 757	6 978	-7 492	21 243	9 863 374
1981-1991	12 111	2 669	-4 298	10 482	9 978 681

Source: NIS, own calculations

Around 1900, this figure had risen to 6.7 million, and by 1992 it was just over 10 million. Approximately 58% of the total population lives in Flanders, 33% in Wallonia and 9% in Brussels. The number of inhabitants per km2 is 325. After the Netherlands, Belgium is the most densely populated country in Europe (the EC average is 150 inhabitants/ km2).

Population growth was very slow over the last few decades; there are only 3.4% more inhabitants in Belgium today than in 1970. There are sharp differences between the Regions here.

POPULATION STATISTICS PER REGION (1991)					
	Number of inhabitants	% of total pop.	Difference from 1970	% of area	Pop. /km²
Brussels Region	954 045	9.56	-121 091	0.53	5 912
Flemish Region	5 768 925	57.81	352 342	44.28	427
Walloon Region	3 255 711	32.63	96 486	55.19	193
Belgium	9 978 681	100.00	327 737	100.00	327

Source: NIS, own calculations

The population of Flanders increased by 6% between 1970 and 1990, while Wallonia showed only a 3% increase and the population of Brussels actually fell by 11%.

* Between 1900 and 1990, the population of Belgium increased by 49%.

* With 14.6% of the total area of Belgium, Luxembourg is the largest province, and also the province with the fewest inhabitants (2.3% of the total population of Belgium in 1990).

BELGIANS & EUROPEANS

Like most other western European countries, Belgium went through a demographic transition at the end of the nineteenth and the beginning of the twentieth century.

In other words, high birth and death rates gave way to low birth and death rates. Mortality was the first to drop, which lead to a substantial population increase. However, this population growth was never explosive in Belgium, where the rate of increase was seldom in excess of 1%. Declining death rates were soon followed by declining birth rates, and moreover, the migration balance was mostly negative during the nineteenth century.

The First World War had a fundamental demographic impact: more people died and fewer children were born. The effects of this are still visible today. But after the war, prewar demographic trends were re-established and natality continued to decline. In the years leading up to the Second World War, the birth rate did not even reach replacement level. World War II also had a profound effect on the number of births and deaths, but after the war the trend was reversed, with a steep rise in births, generally referred to as the "baby boom". This upward trend was to continue right through to the second half of the sixties, when a change again set in.

BELGIUM IN EUROPE (1991)			
	Population ('000)	Area ('000 km²)	Density (inh./km²)
Belgium	**9 987**	**31**	**327**
Denmark	5 146	43	119
Germany (*)	79 700	357	223
(BRD) (**)	(62 700)	(249)	(246)
Greece	10 200	132	77
Spain	38 994	505	77
France	56 893	549	104
Ireland	3 518	70	50
Italy	57 746	301	192
Luxembourg	384	2.6	148
Netherlands	15 010	41	362
Portugal	9 859	92	107
United Kingdom	57 486	244	236
Eur12	344 925	2 368	146

Source: EUROSTAT   (*) situation after 3/10/1990.   (**) situation before 3/10/1990.

AN AGEING POPULATION

A characteristic feature of the present population of Belgium is that the number of young people is declining both numerically and as a proportion of the total population, while the number and proportion of older inhabitants is rising.

Today, almost 2 million inhabitants are over 60 years old, which is three times as many as in 1900. At the beginning of the twentieth century, 10% of the population was over 60; today, it is 20%. The reverse is true of young people. Around 1900, 40% of the population was under 20; that figure is now 25%. This trend is set to continue in the future. It is bound to have important consequences, since virtually all areas of government are affected by a shift in the age structure of the population.

---

* The median age of the Belgian population is 34.7 years (Eur12 = 34.3 years). That means that one in two Belgians are older or younger than 34.7 years.

---

* In 2 000, 17% of the population will be under 15, and 17% will be over 65.

THE BIRTH RATE: A NEW UPSWING?

After World War II, there were 150 000 births per year. The birth rate then rose over the next two decades, peaking in 1964 with 161 000 births.

EVOLUTION OF THE TOTAL FERTILITY RATE

REPLACEMENT LEVEL

Source: N.I.S.

After 1964, the birth rate declined, bottoming out in 1985 at 114 000 births. From 1985 onwards, the natality figures show a slight increase each year. In 1990 there were almost 124 000 births, 56% of which were in Flanders, 34% in Wallonia and 10% in Brussels. The fact that the percentage of births in Brussels is higher than its percentage of the national population is influenced by the large foreign population in the Region.

The decline of the specific fertility rate between 1965 and 1985 is the most marked in the youngest and above all the oldest age groups. For the youngest group, this decline reflects the introduction of efficient methods of contraception, and longer education. The decline among women in the older age groups reflects the fact that fewer women are now producing more than two children. In 1960, 37% of all children born that year were third children. In 1988 this had

dropped to 20%. So not only had the number of births changed, but also their demographic background.

About ten types of contraceptive are in use in Belgium. Over the last two decades there has been a swing from ineffective and sexually unattractive methods to effective and more sexually acceptable methods of contraception. About four out of five women of childbearing age use a contraceptive, putting Belgium at the top of the league in Europe in this respect. The pill, which came on the market in Belgium in 1963, is the most popular method. In 1966, 7% of all fertile women using contraception were taking the pill. By around 1985, this had risen to 40%. Over the same period, sterilization also became more widespread as a method of contraception, while the rhythm method and coitus interruptus in particular declined in popularity.

* The specific fertility rate indicates how many children are born on average per woman, and gives significant information on generation replacement. In developed countries, generation replacement is attained if 210 children are born for every 100 women. This level of births has not been attained in Belgium since 1972. The present rate (approximately 1.6, which is also the European average) is 25% too low to provide for generation replacement.

* The average age at which women in Belgium have their first child is now nearly 26; at the beginning of the seventies it was 24. A small but growing group of women are over 30 when their first child is born.

* The average birth weight of babies born in Belgium is 3 310 grams. Four out of ten weigh in

at between 3100 and 3500 grams. The birth weight of about 7% of babies born in Belgium is low or too low.

* In Belgium, the chance of producing twins is 1 in 110, and for triplets, 1 in 7 000. Since the introduction of a variety of fertility drugs and techniques, the incidence of multiple birth has risen.

* In 1989, 11.0% (Eur 12 = 17.1%) of all babies born were illegitimate; in 1960 extramarital births accounted for 2.1% (Eur 12 = 4.5%).

* Fewer than 1% of all babies are born at home (1960 =13%).

* Over the last few years, fewer than 2% of mothers who have just given birth are under 20 years old; 1% are over 40 years old.

In the sixties, the gross number of deaths was 12 per 1 000; today the figure is 9 per 1 000. In Wallonia and Brussels the death rate is higher because the population is older.

Statistically, the probability of a baby dying during his or her first year of life is the same as that of a 57-year-old man dying before his 58th birthday. The likelihood of death is therefore relatively high among the newborn. Nevertheless, infant mortality has dropped spectacularly over the last three decades. In 1960 it was 31.2 per 1 000 live births (Eur12=34.8) and in 1989 it was 8.6 (Eur12=8.2). After the first year of a baby's life, the likelihood of death decreases, bottoming out at around 10 years of age for boys and 12 for girls. Thereafter, the probability of death increases with age. Approximately 80% of all deaths occur after the age of 60. That is a far higher proportion than in the past. More and more old people are living to a very advanced age, which means that this sector of the population as a whole is aging. In other words, the average age of our senior citizens is increasing. In Belgium, health and retirement costs are already high, and look to be even higher in the future.

A substantial majority of Belgians today (70%) die of

FALLING MORTALITY

Over the last two decades, the annual death rate fluctuated between 104 000 and 120 000.

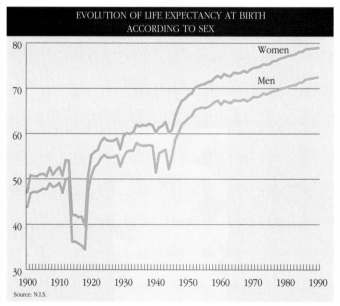

EVOLUTION OF LIFE EXPECTANCY AT BIRTH ACCORDING TO SEX

Source: N.I.S.

cancer or cardiovascular disease. About 44% of all men in Belgium die from the effects of cardiovascular disease; for women, this is 38%. One out of four men and one out of five women die of cancer. The number of deaths in traffic accidents has been about 2000 per annum over the last few years, and the number of suicides 2 300.

Most Belgians have a fairly long lifespan. Men born around the turn of the century could expect to live to the age of 44, and women 47. Today their life expectancy is 71 and 78 respectively. Life expectancy is highest in Flanders and lowest in Wallonia.

* **4% of Belgians know someone in their immediate environment who died in a traffic accident.**

* **The incidence of stillbirth is 5 per 1 000.**

* **Infant mortality is higher among boys than girls, and higher among illegitimate than legitimate children.**

* **The life expectancy of 75-year-old Belgian men is 7.6 years, and 9.8 years for women.**

* **About 15% of all those dying are now cremated; in 1970, that percentage was only 0.5%.**

FOREIGNERS IN BELGIUM

Over the last few decades, more people have come to live in Belgium than have left to live elsewhere.

Immigration peaked in the sixties, reaching its highest level in 1964-66. At this time, Belgium was suffering from a labour shortage, and the government was consequently pursuing an active immigration policy. Since 1974 it has declined, as a result of legal restrictions on immigration and a less favourable economic climate. For decades, there have been more native Belgians leaving the country than returning to it.

In 1992, there were 922 500 foreign nationals in Belgium, amounting to 9% of the total population. The European average is 3.9%. The largest section of this foreign population lives in the Walloon Region (42%), with 30% in the Brussels Region and 28% in the Flemish Region. Brussels has the highest concentration of foreign immigrants: 28% of the population is non-Belgian; in Wallonia that figure is 11%, and in Flanders 4%. In 1970, these figures were lower. There are not only more foreign-

ers today, but they also represent a larger proportion of the population as a whole. The various nationalities represented among the foreign population also show a shift in emphasis over the years. The proportion of immigrants from EC countries has declined in comparison with those from Morocco and Turkey. These are precisely the groups where the social and cultural gap is the greatest.

---

* **By far the greatest majority of Belgians emigrating, do so to other European countries.**

---

* **One marriage in ten in Belgium is ethnically mixed.**

---

* **There are 321 000 non-EC subjects; that represents 37% of the foreign population and 3% of the total population.**

---

* **After Luxembourg, Belgium has the highest proportion of foreigners in the population of all the EC Member Countries.**

FOREIGNERS IN BELGIUM (1992)			
	Number of foreigners	% of foreigners	% of population of the Region
Brussels Region	276 459	30.0	29.1
Flemish Region	268 901	29.1	4.6
Walloon Region	377 142	40.9	11.5
Total	922 502	100.0	9.2

Source: NIS, own calculations

FOREIGNERS ACCORDING TO NATIONALITY (1991)

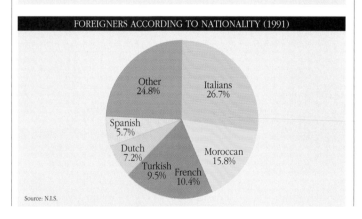

Source: N.I.S.

MARRIAGES

Between 1960 and 1970, almost everyone got married; today about two out of three do so.

So what was almost universal in the sixties is now still the custom of the majority, but there is also a substantial minority who remain unmarried. Between 1970 and 1988, enthusiasm for marriage cooled dramatically right across the country, but since 1988 there has been an upturn in the number of people getting married. Most marriages are celebrated with parties for family and friends on a grand scale.

Most Belgians have both a civil marriage and a church wedding. The majority only feel that they are truly married after their union has been consecrated in a church ceremony. In 1967, 86% of all civil weddings were followed by a religious ceremony; in 1989 this was only 60%. These percentages include couples barred from a church wedding because at least one of the partners is divorced. If we consider only couples eligible to marry in church, we find that 20% of them do not do so today, as against 6% in 1967. In other words, one in six couples planning to marry opt for a civil ceremony only.

In recent years, a clear distinction has emerged between first-time marriages and remarriage. Around 1970, remarriages accounted for 10% of all weddings; today that figure is 24%. In Brussels it is as high as 30%. But although the number of second (or subsequent) marriages rose, there was an overall trend away from remarrying. Between 1890 and 1975, about 70% of all divorcees remarried. Since 1976, that percentage has declined to 40 or 45% today, and for widows and widowers it is under 10%.

The trend away from remarriage is linked to the growing popularity of cohabitation without marriage. An estimated one in ten Belgians has had some experience of cohabitation. And this includes not only unmarried young people today, but also divorcees, widows and widowers. Research has shown that 45% of divorcees remarry within 5 years of their divorce, and that 25% cohabit with a permanent partner.

---

* Around 1980, 75% of the Belgian population did not agree with the statement that marriage is an obsolete institution.

---

* The average age of those marrying for the first time in 1989 was 26 years and 1 month for men and 24 years and 1 month for women.

---

* The average age of those remarrying is 40 years 1 month for men and 36 years 11 months for women.

---

* The festive character of a Belgian wedding is reflected by the fact that there are three times as many weddings per day in July as in January.

AND MORE COUPLES ARE GETTING DIVORCED

In 1960 there were 4 600 divorces in Belgium, as against 20 800 in 1991. This represents a fourfold increase within one generation, both in absolute terms and as a proportion of the population.

These figures do not include the separation of unmarried couples living together. Between a quarter and a third of all marriages entered into in Belgium today will end in divorce. This proportion is higher in Brussels (1987: 37%) than in Flanders (23%) or Wallonia (28%). Since 1981, new marriages have been outnumbered by marriages terminated (by divorce or death) : something which has never happened before. Over the last few years, married couples have represented a smaller and smaller proportion of the population.

The rising divorce rate naturally has a profound effect on the children involved. Today's statistics indicate that the parants of 1% of all Belgian minors will divorce per calendar year. One in ten of the present younger generation will see their parents, whether married or not, separating or divorcing. This is a process which is often fraught with problems, and for this reason,

Belgium has set up a number of guidance services and provisions to help both the children and their parents as much as possible.

* **Out of all couples who married in 1955, 1% divorced within 5 years (i.e. before 1960); among couples who married in 1988 it was 5%.**

* **The median lifespan of**

marriages ending in divorce was 12 years and 9 months in 1990. The median age on divorce was 37 years and 3 months for men, and 35 years for women.

* **In 1960, 82% of divorces were declared on specified grounds, and 18% by mutual consent; today, those figures are 55% and 45% respectively.**

* **Since the beginning of the eighties, more marriages have been dissolved in Belgium by divorce than through the death of the wife.**

FAMILIES

*On 1 March 1991, when the last census was taken,
there were 3 953 000 households
in Belgium.*

The average number of people living together in each family was just under three. At the beginning of the last century it was five. This downturn can be explained by the falling birth rate, a longer lifespan, fewer first and subsequent marriages, and a higher divorce rate.

One of the most striking developments of the last few decades is the substantial increase in the number and proportion of people living alone. In 1970 18.8% of all households were people living alone; in 1981 that had risen to 23.2%, and 28.4% in 1991. The ageing of the population is one of the causal factors here, but another factor is certainly the increasing preference for living independently.

Another significant development is the increased number of one-parent families. This can be attributed mainly to the increasing number of divorces, and to the fact that people are less likely to

remarry today. However, care should be taken when interpreting these statistics, since many people live together after divorce without marrying, and this does not figure in the official records.

* **Single-parent families in Belgium represent 7% of all families (1981)**

* **In Brussels, one child in six under 18 lives in a single-parent family; in Flanders that is one in fifteen and in Wallonia one in nine (statistics for 1981).**

* **9% of the families in Belgium have five or more members.**

* **Less than 1% of Belgian households comprise two or more nuclear families.**

* **One in four Belgian households have a cat, and one in three a dog. This puts Belgium at the top of the European league in this respect.**

THE VARIOUS TYPES OF FAMILY AS A % OF THE TOTAL POPULATION

	1970	1981	1991
Man living alone	6.4	8.4	11.8
Woman living alone	12.4	14.7	16.6
Nuclear families			
- married couple without children	24.3	23.5	n.k.
- mar. couple with unmar. children	39.9	38.6	n.k.
- father with unmarried children	1.1	1.1	n.k.
- mother with unmarried children	4.1	4.8	n.k.
Extended families			
- married couple without children	1.9	1.4	n.k.
- mar. couple with unmar. children	3.8	2.2	n.k.
- father with unmarried children	0.4	0.3	n.k.
- mother with unmarried children	0.9	0.8	n.k.
Other	4.8	4.2	n.k.
Total (in thousands)	3 234	3 608	3 953

Source: NIS

HOUSING

There are about 3 900 000 homes in Belgium.

HOUSING IN THE EUROPEAN COMMUNITY (1989, AS A PERCENTAGE)		
	Belgium	Eur 12
Single-family house (owner-occupied)	65	48
Flat (owner-occupied)	3	14
Single-family house (rented)	20	12
Flat (rented)	11	24
Other	1	2
No answer	0	1

Source: Eurobarometer

HOME STATISTICS		
	1981	1991
Average number of residents per home	2.7	2.6
Average number of rooms per home	5.03	4.3
Average number of rooms per resident	1.85	1.7
Average area per home	82.12 m²	86.29 m²
Average area per resident	30.14 m²	34.00 m²

Source: NIS

COMFORT IN THE HOME (AS A PERCENTAGE)			
	1970	1981	1991
Central heating	29.6	51.3	60.1
Bathroom or shower	49.0	76.1	87.7
Telephone	36.0	61.9	/
Indoor flush W.C.	52.6	81.3	92.0
Insulation	/	27.1	/
Mains water supply	89.8	98.0	99.0
Kitchen minimum 4 m²	84.2	83.4	/

Source: NIS

The majority of these homes (96%) are in buildings comprising more than one residential unit (flats, etc.). In Flanders, 65% of homes are owner-occupied; in Wallonia this is 63% and in Brussels 31%. More than half the homes in Flanders were built after the second world war, while in Wallonia half of all housing was built over 75 years ago. Comfort in the home has increased substantially over the last decades.

THE BATTLE AGAINST DISEASE

In 1960, global expenditure on health care in Belgium amounted to 3.4% of GNP; in 1990 it had risen to 7.2%.

This reflects the heavy investment in the health sector and the development of an extensive range of services offering curative and preventive care. Health care in Belgium is now of a very high standard. However, serious challenges still remain. In 1989, a representative sample of the Belgian population were asked what they considered to be the most serious threat to the health of the nation. Cancer and Aids figured prominently among their answers.

Today, in 1990, almost all children have been immunised against polio, diphtheria and tetanus, and 75% against whooping cough. Measles vaccinations have been available free of charge since 1985, resulting in a sharp decline in the incidence of the disease. In Flanders, 80% are vaccinated against measles, and 40% in Wallonia.

The number of people suffering a heart attack is estimated at about 40 000 a year. The probability of a heart attack increases with age: 50% of all heart attacks occur among the over-seventies. In all age groups, there are more heart attacks among men than women. In one case in five the attack causes sudden death. There are 100 000 registered cases of cancer. That means that 1% of the population is presently suffering from cancer. The number of new cases of cancer is an important indicator of public health. According to the National Cancer Register, there are about 35 000 new cases of malignant tumours each year, 18 000 of which are men and 17 000 women. That is 370 for every 100 000 men and 330 for every 100 000 women. According to the statistics of the Institute of Hygiene and Epidemiology, there are between 50 000 and 55 000 new cases of cancer every year, 54% of which are in men. Lung cancer is the most frequent form of cancer in men, and breast cancer in women.

A recent survey indicated that four out of five Belgians felt that their health was worth spending on. In 1988, expenditure on health accounted for 11% of total household expenditure (6.8% in 1970). A striking feature is the fairly frequent consumption of foods with a high sugar, fat and salt content. Consumption of salt-free and sugar-free products is low: only 5% of the population use them occasionally, and users are more often women than men. Consumption of these products increases with age, indicating that consumers switch to dietary products primarily on medical advice. Organically grown produce enjoys increasing popularity (10% of the population), particularly among younger consumers.

* **Over the last century, Belgian men are 7 cm taller on average, and women 5 cm. Between 1925 and 1960, the average height of three-year-old boys has increased by 3 cm, and that of 15-year-olds by 10 cm. The average height of young Belgian men today is 1.76 m, and 1.60 m for women. Adult men have an average weight of 75 kg, and women 60 kg. Over the last decade, men have become 3 kg heavier on average, while women weigh an average of 0.5 kg less. Just over 5% of the Belgian population (8% of women, 3% of men) has used a slimming product at some time.**

ALCOHOL CONSUMPTION

One Belgian in six drinks at least one glass of beer a day; 40% never or almost never drink beer.

Between 1960 and 1980, total alcohol consumption rose steadily in Belgium, primarily in the form of spirits and wine. Beer consumption remained fairly stable. Since 1980, consumption of alcoholic beverages other than wine has stabilised or even decreased. Wine consumption per head of population was 7.8 litres in 1960, as against 24.9 litres in 1990. In 1960 the per capita consumption of pure alcohol from spirits was 0.77 litre; in 1990 it was 1.20 litre. The highest beer consumption was clocked up in 1973 at 143 litres per capita. By 1990 it had fallen to 121 litres. Taking all alcoholic beverages together, Belgians consume an average of 10 litres of pure alcohol per year (1990). In other words, alcohol accounts for 1.5% of total expenditure on housekeeping.

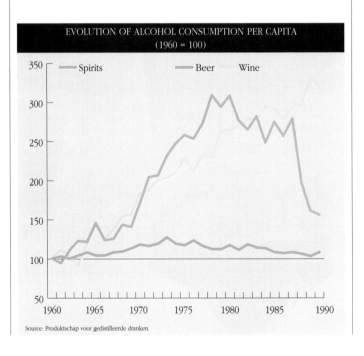

EVOLUTION OF ALCOHOL CONSUMPTION PER CAPITA
(1960 = 100)

Spirits   Beer   Wine

Source: Produktschap voor gedistilleerde dranken

* One Belgian in six drinks at least one glass of beer a day; 40% never or almost never drink beer.

* Young adults drink more and more often than older adults. The 25-34 age group scores highest on both counts.

* Both men and women drink more beer at home than outside.

* The number of Belgians who drink too much is estimated at 300 000. That corresponds to 4% of the population over the age of 15. Excessive drinkers are those who consume at least 15 cl of pure alcohol per day.

TOBACCO CONSUMPTION

In 1991, 25% of the population in Flanders were regular smokers, as were 33% in Wallonia and 29% in Brussels.

Ceci n'est pas une pipe.

© Magritte, Sabam

In the sixties, about 45% of the adult population were smokers (70% of men, 20% of women). Over the last two decades these figures have decreased, at least for men. Today, there are still 29% of the population smoking on a daily basis (33% men, 24% women). This downturn can be attributed to the anti-smoking movement's campaigns. One of the movement's achievements was the Royal Decree of 31 March 1987 prohibiting smoking in public places. There is also a growing proportion of young people who have never smoked, and the number of ex-smokers is increasing.

* **An average of 1.6% of the total housekeeping budget is spent on tobacco.**

* **30% of all deaths from cancer are caused by smoking.**

* **In 1988, 18.2 billion cigarettes were sold in Belgium and Luxembourg combined.**

* **20% of all pregnant women remain active smokers throughout pregnancy.**

* **The percentage of women who smoke increases with their level of education; the reverse is true of men.**

MEDICAL CARE

In 1950 there was one doctor for every 800 inhabitants; today there is one for every 300. The number of consultations per doctor also decreased significantly. In 1975 the average doctor in Flanders had 220 consultations per week; today he has only 130. In Wallonia and Brussels the figure is even lower. The growing number of doctors was a key factor in this evolution, since the average number of times an individual consults his or her GP has remained stable at around four to five times a year.

The number of dentists also increased substantially. In 1960 there were 5 700 people for every dentist, and 1 400 in 1990. Over the last few years, dentists were the fastest-growing group in the medical sector. This led to a decline in the number of treatments performed per dentist. One half of the population claim to be aware that a check-up every six months is ideal to keep one's teeth healthy. However, only half of the population visits the dentist at least once a year, and almost one in three had failed to do so in the last five years.

The number of doctors quadrupled between 1960 and 1990.

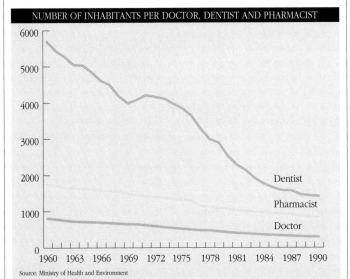

NUMBER OF INHABITANTS PER DOCTOR, DENTIST AND PHARMACIST

Dentist
Pharmacist
Doctor

Source: Ministry of Health and Environment

The number of pharmacists showed the slowest growth rate over the last decades. Their numbers have increased, but not as explosively as for doctors and dentists. There are still 800 inhabitants per pharmacist today, as against 1 700 in 1960.

* **In 1987, an average of eight medicines were prescribed per person per year in Belgium, 29 in France and 6 in Denmark.**

* **Approximately 75% of general medical costs (provided or prescribed by a GP) are refunded through the (compulsory) medical insurance system.**

* **In 1986 there were 4.7 non-psychiatric and 2.1 psychiatric hospital beds per 1 000 inhabitants.**

* **In Belgium, there is one physiotherapist for every 600 inhabitants.**

* **Over-the-counter sales of medication (without a prescription) account for 24% of all sales of medicines.**

DENSITY OF MEDICAL STAFF (1987, PER 100 000 INHABITANTS)			
	Doctors	Dentists	Pharmacists
Italy	111	13	/
United Kingdom	137	35	/
Ireland	141	34	31
Luxembourg	179	49	74
Netherlands	235	52	14
France	249	65	88
Denmark	256	93	29
Portugal	257	8	100
West Germany	280	63	55
Belgium	**321**	**63**	**112**
Greece	333	91	66
Spain	338	15	80

Source: EUROSTAT

HEALTH & FITNESS

Physical culture is an important part of life in Belgium today, just as in other Western European countries.

A good 10% of the family budget is spent on toiletries and bodycare products. Popular magazines focusing explicitly or implicitly on physical culture achieve high circulation figures. Amateur sport and all kinds of physical activities are popular among the general public. The common aim is: "a healthy mind in a healthy body". This target is reflected in the lively market for slimming aids of all kinds: almost 10% of all Belgian women (and 3% of men) have used a slimming aid at least once. Obesity increases with age, but the young put more effort into staying slim. Certain statistics indicate that in Belgium, one man in four and one woman in five is overweight.

THE ORGANIZATION OF EDUCATION

Education in Belgium remained a national affair for a long period of time, with a centralist, bureaucratic organization.

In fact, it combined all the characteristic features of a typically Belgian bone of contention. In the previous century, tension had already built up between the Liberals and Socialists on the one side, and the Catholics on the other. The former were in favour of state education, while the latter wanted both to exert their influence in state education and extend their own Catholic education network at the same time. Political feeling ran high on this subject, and the so-called "school question" and led to a succession of passionate clashes. One of these erupted during the "second school war" (1954-58), at a time when there was a Liberal-Socialist coalition government. In a nutshell, the problem was that the "free" (ie. Catholic) schools did not receive adequate state subsidies and therefore had to charge tuition fees, while there were not enough state schools to allow all parents to exercise their freedom of choice in practice. Negotiations finally led to the signing of the School Pact on 20 November 1958. The pact covered all branches of education except the universities. Its basic principles are free education to the age of 18, and freedom of choice for parents in selecting a school for their children. In practical terms this meant the expansion of the state educa-

tion network and also substantial subsidies for the non-state network.

However, tension between Flanders and Wallonia dragged on, fuelled by conflicts over education, and on 1 January 1989 responsibility for education was finally handed over to the Communities. This made the system more flexible, so that Regional education authorities could respond directly to specific local

requests and requirements. This move towards a smaller-scale, decentralised approach also gave schools more autonomy. But at the same time, there is also a trend in the opposite direction. The creation of a single internal market for Europe from 1993, with free movement of goods and persons, means that European authorities have a greater impact on education policies. There are two groups of initiators in the

organization of education in Belgium: private and public. The initiators of public education are the Municipalities, Provinces and Communities. There are three education networks: Community Education (with 17% of the pupils in 1988-89), Independent Subsidised Education, which is mainly Catholic (60% of the pupils) and Official Subsidised Education, 3% of which is organized by the Provinces and 19% by the Municipalities. Education is compulsory between the ages of 6 and 18 (a total of 12 years), and may be preceded by optional pre-school kindergarten. Primary education lasts six years, followed by six years of secondary education. Secondary education starts at the age of 12, and is divided into three "grades", each lasting two years. The first year of the first grade is in principle the same for all streams. From the second year onwards, the number of options increases. Secondary education comprises general secondary education, technical secondary education, secondary art education and secondary vocational education. A recent amendment now allows many schools a certain degree of freedom to set up their curriculum as they see fit. Higher education comprises university and non-university higher education.

INVESTING IN KNOWLEDGE

In every industrialised society, education has a crucial role to play.

In every industrialised society, education plays a crucial role in passing on attitudes, skills and knowledge. It is sometimes said that "grey matter" is the only real raw material in Belgium. Postwar educational policy aimed explicitly at raising the educational level of the population and democratising education in general. Financial barriers were broken down: primary and secondary education is free, and a wide-ranging system of grants and maintenance allowances has been set up.

The level of education has risen appreciably over the last few decades. This was more marked among girls than boys; the participation gap between girls and boys

has narrowed, and in recent years, the percentage of girls still at school at 15 and 18 has actually been higher than the percentage of boys of the same age. Boys are still overrepresented among 21-year-old students, but this gap is closing too. The Belgian authorities are investing heavily in quality education. On 29 June 1983 a law was passed raising the school-leaving age from 14 to 18 (full-time schooling up to the age of 16, and parttime from 16-18). Belgian pupils and students spend considerably more hours per week in the classroom than their fellow students in the rest of Europe. The ratio of teachers to every 1 000 inhabitants is also high in Belgium.

TIME SPENT IN THE CLASSROOM (HOURS PER YEAR) IN PRIMARY AND SECONDARY EDUCATION		
	Primary	Secondary
Belgium	**950**	**1 216-1 368**
Denmark	540-780	1 080
Spain	875	1 085
France	972	1 067
Greece	603-658	1 020
Ireland	805-897	1 050-1 170
Italy	792-864	1 080
Luxembourg	954	954
Netherlands	660-768	1 120-1 148
Portugal	750-860	1 056-1 120
West Germany	600-780	1 280
United Kingdom	560-620	1 080

Source: Les Systèmes Educatifs en Europe

NUMBER OF TEACHERS PER GRADE (1988, PER 1000 INHABITANTS)			
	1st & 2nd year	3rd & 4th year	5th & 6th year
Belgium	**6.9**	**10.5**	**2.0**
Denmark	6.7	6.1	/
Spain	/	/	/
France	4.3	7.3	1.1
Greece	3.8	5.2	1.2
Ireland	4.5	5.8	1.7
Italy	/	/	/
Luxembourg	/	/	/
Netherlands	5.8	6.8	/
Portugal	6.9	4.0	/
West Germany	2.2	6.6	3.0
United Kingdom	3.8	7.1	1.4

Source: Unesco

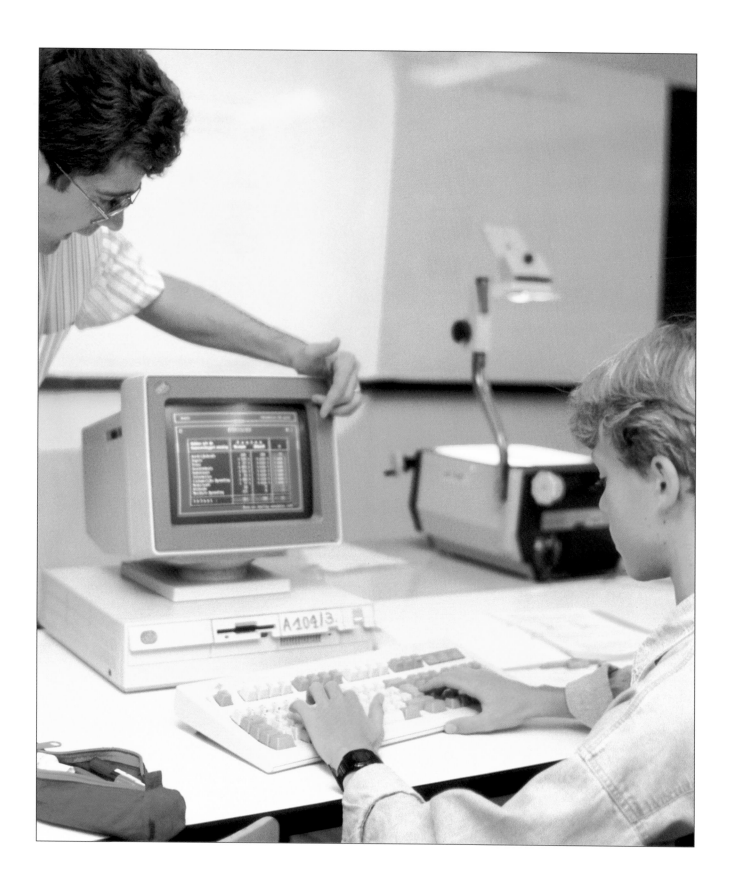

*Students
at the new
university town
Louvain-la-Neuve*

HIGHER EDUCATION

Encouraged by financial incentives from the government, participation in higher education has grown dramatically over the last two decades.

Between 1970-71 and 1990-91 the number of students in Dutch language higher non-university education increased by 121%, and the number of university students by 64%. Growth in French language and German language higher education over the same period was 76% and 36% respectively.

Education is not the only function of Belgian universities. They also carry out pure and applied research, increasingly in the context of an international network of universities and research institutes. Industry is investing more and more in research and training. One in two companies in Belgium have a special budget for training. Almost three-quarters of total expenditure on research and development in Belgium comes from industry.

From being a manufacturing-based society, Belgium is now evolving into a knowledge-based society. That is why investing in education is so important. More knowledge goes into making a computer or hi-tech medical equipment than raw materials. But technical knowledge soon becomes out of date, and the student's original degree or diploma cannot meet the knowledge requirements of the future. Consequently, there is a strong focus on permanent education today. In 1991, permanent education was specifically named as one of the educational tasks of the universities. It is also stimulated by the EC.

* **There are 19 universities and university institutions in Belgium.**

* **Almost 13% of university students in Belgium are of non-Belgian nationality. The Dutch language universities have 5% foreign students, and the French-speaking universities 20%.**

* **There are 40 scientific researchers for every 10 000 employees in Belgium, as against 87 in Japan and 11 in Portugal.**

* **In Belgium, 1.4% of total expenditure on wages in business and industry goes on training; in France this is 2.7%.**

Papal college in Leuven

SCIENTIFIC RESEARCH

Various Belgian university research institutes are among the world leaders in scientific research.

One of these is the Inter-University Microelectronics Center (IMEC), set up in Leuven in 1984, where hundreds of researchers are now working on chip technology. It is one of the most modern laboratories in the world for fundamental research in this field. The Centrum voor Menselijke Erfelijkheid (Human Genetics Centre) of the Catholic University of Leuven has also won international renown for its work on genetic engineering. Plant Genetic Systems (PGS) of the State University of Ghent also enjoys an international reputation. This is a biotechnology enterprise set up in 1982 as an integral part of the Genetics Laboratory. It won the attention of the international scientific world with its achievements in developing insect-resistant plants. The University of Ghent also has one of the largest bacteria banks in Europe. The University of

Antwerp leads the field with its research on the electron structure of materials and laser applications.

The Department of Space Research of the State University of Liège is a renowned laboratory which works in close cooperation with the European Space Agency (ESA). Scientists at the Institute of Cellular and Molecular Pathology of the Catholic University of Louvain-la-Neuve develop applications in the field of medical examination and treatment for the results of their fundamental biological research. The Department of Molecular Biology of the University of Brussels is active in the field of genetic engineering. The Institute of Interface Science of the Faculté Notre-Dame de la Paix in Namur makes an international contribution to the development of industrial applications for microelectronics.

BELGIAN NOBEL PRIZE WINNERS

Of the nine Nobel prizes won by Belgium so far, five have been in the scientific sector.

BORDET, Jules Jean Baptiste Vincent
Prize: Medicine and physiology, 1919, for his discoveries in the field of immunity.
Born: 13 June 1870, in Soignies - Died: 6 April 1961, in Brussels.

CLAUDE, Albert
Prize: Medicine and physiology, 1974, for his contribution to the understanding of the structure and function of the internal components of cells (together with C. De Duve).
Born: 24 August 1898, in Luxembourg - Died: 22 May 1983, in Brussels.

de DUVE, Christian René Marie Joseph
Prize: Medicine and physiology, 1974, for his contribution to the understanding of the structure and function of the internal components of cells (together with A. Claude).
Born: 2 October 1917, Thames Ditton, United Kingdom

HEYMANS, Corneille Jean François
Prize: Medicine and physiology, 1938, for his work on the role of sinuses and arteries in the regulation of respiration.
Born: 28 March 1892, in Ghent - Died: 18 July 1968, in Knokke

PRIGOGINE, Ilya
Prize: Chemistry, 1977, for his revolutionary theory of dissipative ("wasteful") structures.
Born: 25 January 1917, in Moscow, Russia.

Biotechnology research at PGS in Ghent (RUG)

RELIGION

Approximately three in four Belgians describe themselves as Catholics (in the broadest sense of the word). In Flanders that is 76% and 66% in Wallonia.

The remaining one in four Belgians include about 10% "doubters" and 12% free-thinkers; almost half are firmly-convinced free-thinkers. Between 1.5 and 2% of the population are followers of Islam (ie. 150 000 people). They are mainly immigrants from the Maghreb countries and Turkey, and most of them live in Brussels. One percent of the population is Protestant; half of them belong to the United Protestant Church in Belgium, and the other half are members of various Free Churches and sects. One of these Protestant sects are the Jehovah's Wit-

nesses, with an estimated membership of 20 000. Another relatively large religious minority are the Jews, who have about 35 000 members.

WHAT DO YOU BELIEVE IN ? (AS A PERCENTAGE, 1990)						
	God	Life after death	Hell	Heaven	Resurrection	Reincarnation
France	57	38	16	30	27	24
Great Britain	71	44	25	53	32	24
West Germany	64	38	13	31	31	19
Netherlands	61	39	14	34	27	15
Belgium	**63**	**37**	**15**	**30**	**27**	**13**
Denmark	59	29	8	17	20	15
Sweden	38	31	7	27	19	17
Norway	58	36	39			
Iceland	79	71	11	51	44	32
Italy	84	54	36	45	44	22
Spain	81	42	27	48	34	20
Portugal	80	31	21	49	31	23
Northern Ireland	90	70	68	86	71	30
Republic of Ireland	96	78	50	85	70	19
U.S.A.	93	70	5	81	65	22
Canada	86	61	38	67	50	27

Source: Europees Waardenonderzoek

RELIGION IN BELGIUM (1990, %)	
Catholic	75.0
-regular churchgoer	23.0
-non-churchgoer	52.0
Free-thinkers	12.0
-firmly-held conviction	5.0
-nominal free-thinker	7.0
Islamic	1.5
Protestant	1.0
Jewish	0.3
Other religion or sect	0.2
No religion/doubters	10.0

Source: Department of Religious and Cultural Sociology, Catholic University of Leuven

PRACTISING BELIEVERS

Every religion attempts to express through rituals both the bond linking the members of that faith and their bond with a "Higher Being".

These ritual practices are the visible and measurable features of a religion in society. Within the Catholic Church, the most important rites are Sunday Mass, baptism, the funeral service, marriage service and confession. The number of regular churchgoers, ie. those who attend a Eucharist every week, has been gradually declining since 1964. Around 1950, one in two Catholics attended Sunday Mass regularly; today that is only one in five. The largest group now comprises those who still regard themselves as Catholic, but only go to church for special occa-

WHAT DO PEOPLE CONSIDER TO BE (VERY) IMPORTANT IN LIFE ? (IN %, 1990)						
	Work	Family	Friends	Leisure time	Politics	Religion
France	92	97	86	80	32	42
Great Britain	76	97	92	86	43	31
West Germany	78	88	88	83	41	36
Netherlands	90	92	95	90	53	44
Belgium	**89**	**95**	**90**	**85**	**25**	**45**
Denmark	90	98	93	89	43	31
Sweden	96	96	97	95	45	27
Norway	96	99	97	92	50	40
Iceland	91	98	92	83	26	56
Italy	95	99	91	82	30	69
Spain	93	98	91	82	20	54
Portugal	94	97	83	75	21	56
Northern Ireland	81	99	95	79	28	67
Republic of Ireland	91	98	94	80	28	84
U.S.A.	86	98	93	86	51	79
Canada	88	99	94	88	48	61

Source: Europees Waardenonderzoek

sions. In Flanders, attendance at Mass is higher than in Wallonia and Brussels, but even in Flanders, the decline in attendance figures has accelerated over recent years. In 1968, one person in two went to Mass regulary on Sunday, whereas that is only true of one in four today. In Wallonia, one in three went regulary to Sunday Mass in 1968, as against one in five today. Confession has also declined. Over a third of practising believers in Belgium do not confess once a year, and out of those who do confess, only half do so in a personal confession.

LEISURE & PLEASURE

LEISURE

*Just as in other western
European countries, the people
of Belgium have more and
more leisure time.*

All together, including Saturdays and Sundays, paid Bank Holidays (10 per year), holidays (at least 20 days per year) and a variety of other days off, this amounts to 150 non-working days per year. There are as many hours of pure leisure as are spent on job-related activities. The week (168 hours) is divided up on average as follows: 60 hours sleep, 40 hours work, 34 hours semi-leisure time (cooking, eating etc.) and 34 hours pure leisure time.

Spending on leisure activities continues to increase. Approximately one fifth of available income is spent on leisure activities in the broadest sense of the word, making it the third largest category, after housing and food. There are striking differences between the social classes here. The higher the income, the larger the proportion spent on leisure activities. Farmers spend 10% of their income on leisure; among those who are not economically active, manual workers, traders, white collar workers, employers and those in the liberal professions it is higher. These last three groups spend more on leisure activities than on food.

LEISURE ACTIVITIES

People today enjoy more free time than in the past, and the quality of their leisure activities has also changed for the better.

Many factors have contributed to this: increased purchasing power is one of them, and demographic changes like the aging of the population and the growing group of wealthy senior citizens. Foreign travel to distant countries, adventure and amusement parks are increasingly within the reach of ordinary people.

A large proportion of leisure time is spent watching television. The average Flemish viewer spends an average of 135 minutes a day watching television, and the average person in Wallonia 150 minutes. Men clock up about the same number of hours as women. The higher the educational level of the viewer, the less time he spends watching television. Pensioners and the unemployed spend between half an hour and one hour longer watching television than the average Flemish viewer. Manual workers watch more than white collar workers and the self-employed.

On average, people in Flanders listen to the radio for four hours a day, both during the week and at the weekend. Women listen more than men, and young people more than their elders.

In the commercial entertainment category, cafés/pubs and restaurants are the most popular venues, with 72% and 62% respectively (figures for 1983). Funfairs, annual shows and markets also attract about 60% of the population.

Another type of leisure activity is membership of a club of some kind. There are professional clubs and socio-cultural clubs, sports, hobby, political and young people's clubs and associations. In 1983 43% of the Flemish population between 15 and 64 years old was a member of one or more associations. In 1963 it was even 70%.

THE BELGIANS

READING

Approximately 85% of all people in Flanders read a newspaper at least sometimes; one in two do so every day.

Seven out of ten Flemings read a magazine of some kind now and then, women more often than men, and young people more than their elders. Only about half of them ever read a book. This is closely linked with age and education: people read less and less as they grow older, and the higher their education, the more they read.

Redu, the "Village of Books", is a small village in Wallonia with barely 400 inhabitants. But it does have 23 bookshops, 10 craft workshops, 5 art galleries and about 10 little cafés. Every year this little village celebrates its new lease of life with a Book Weekend, when it welcomes second-hand book dealers and everyone interested in their wares.

HOBBIES & GAMES

Over the last twenty years, interest in hobbies of various kinds has increased sharply, because people have more time for them nowadays. This is particularly true of women. Also, many of today's hobbies were formerly regarded as semi-leisure activities.

Approximately two out of every three Flemings (from 15 - 64 years of age) occasionally play a board or card game. Card games are the most popular. One in ten have played a quiz game at least once, and about the same number of people play chess or video games. About one in six play the occasional game of draughts. In the commercial entertainment category, cafés/pubs and restaurants are the most popular venues, with 72% and 62% respectively (figures for 1983). Funfairs, annual shows and markets also attract about 60% of the population.

GASTRONOMY

Belgians have always been among the leading lights in the field of gastronomy. Flemish Benedictines invented beer. Charles de l'Ecluse, a Fleming generally known as Clusius, played an important part in the introduction of the potato all over Europe.

Old cookery books often contain references to Belgium, and today Belgium is still among the leaders of modern haute cuisine. Belgium has as many Michelin stars per head of population as France !

The gastronomic delights of Belgium enjoy international fame. Throughout the country, there are excellent restaurants dedicated to the art of fine eating. Local dishes figure prominently on the menu. On the coast, the most prized dishes are those featuring North Sea fish and shellfish. Thousands of restaurants great and small prepare the harvest of the sea in every way known to man. The Ardennes are famous above all for their fresh trout and crayfish.

As far as meat is concerned, beef, pork and lamb are the most popular. In the hunting season, venison and wild boar are served in various forms in forested regions like the Ardennes. And partridge, pheasant, quail, rabbit and hare are served all over Belgium. Local ingredients are often combined with foreign produce for these dishes.

Traditional dishes made from ancient recipes are also famous, such as Gentse Waterzooi (a kind of chicken stew), Vlaamse Stoverij (stewed meat in a sauce often prepared with brown beer), eel in green sauce (with parsley, lemon and a variety of herbs) and rabbit with prunes.

The national drink of Belgium is beer. Countless breweries produce a vast range of popular beers, and a number of monasteries brew the famous Patersbier (eg. Orval and Westmalle). Belgium ranks among the world leaders for both production and consumption of beer. The number of different Belgian beers is estimated at between 350 and 600. Nowhere in the world will you find such a rich variety. "Belgium, Beer Paradise" is no empty slogan !

There are also about 80 different types of cheese, proportionally more than in France, the Netherlands and Switzerland combined.

And of course, Belgian chocolates are reputed to be the best in the world. There are more than 400 different kinds. Then there are countless varieties of cakes, pancakes, gateaux and tarts, as well as the famous Brussels and Liège waffles.

Carnival in Fosse

CARNIVAL

*In Wallonia the ancient
tradition of carnival lives on,
not as an artificial attraction
for outsiders, but as an authentic
folk event carefully prepared
over the months before
Lent by the people themselves,
in the family circle and
carnival associations.*

In Stavelot, the carnival parade is held halfway through Lent. A great number of groups take part in the parade, which dates back to the year 1499, according to the inhabitants of this little town in the Ardennes. In that year, a new Abbot was appointed to the local abbey, and he forbade the monks to join in the townspeople's mid-Lent celebrations. As a protest, the people of Stavelot dressed up in monk's habit, their faces hidden behind a mask with a long nose. They are referred to here as "Blancs Moussis" - "those clothed in white". It was the students above all who breathed new life into the carnival at Stavelot, bringing back the traditional carnival "giants", confetti canons, pig's bladders and long-handled brooms of ages past.

The 40 Melons in Namur

In Malmédy, carnival - or "Cwarmé" as it is called there - is a tradition which goes back centuries. It has ten or more special carnival characters, the most famous of which is Haguette. He wears a two-cornered hat decorated with colourful ostrich feathers and a brown velvet costume with golden fringes. He keeps his face hidden behind a piece of plain material, and tries to grab the arms and legs of unsuspecting spectators with wooden tongs, refusing to release them until they beg for forgiveness.

The carnival in Binche is famous all over Europe, and often copied both in Belgium and abroad. At the break of dawn on Shrove Tuesday, the drummer fetches the "Gilles" from their homes, and strikes up the rhythm of the dance they will keep up for 24 hours. It is an intoxicating rhythm which soon has everyone on his feet and joining in. The Gilles wear a costume made from a full five metres of magnificent material, decorated with twelve heraldic lions, 150 metres of white ribbon, lace and a belt hung with tinkling copper bells. For the last dance on the market-place in Binche, the Gilles put on their famous hat: a crown with eight gigantic ostrich feathers which wave to the rhythm of the dance, beckoning the spectators to come and join them. An unforgettable spectacle !

Carnival in Flanders shares many similarities with carnival in Germany. It is celebrated in Maaseik, Tongeren, Hasselt, Genk and Aalst, as well as other towns. The carnival in Aalst is one of the best in Belgium. Starting on the last Sunday before

Lent, it is a popular event with almost everyone entering into the spirit. A long procession accompanies the town "giants" and "Ros Balatum", which is a parody of the legendary Ros Beiaard of Dendermonde. Legend has it that a huge horse, the Ros Beiaard, ridden by the four Heemskinderen, played an important part in the battle between Charlemagne and one of his vassals. Later, a prisoner in Dendermonde made a model of the horse's head. Everyone thought it was magnificent and determined that it should remain unique. So to make sure that the prisoner never made another one, his eyes were put out. Ever since, the Ros Beiaard has been jealously guarded in Den-

dermonde. When Aalst demanded the horse's head, Dendermonde naturally refused to part with it, so the people of Aalst made their own variation: the Ros Balatum.

In Geraardsbergen in the southern corner of East Flanders, the ancient tradition of the "Tonnekensbrand" is still observed on the first Sunday in Lent. At two o'clock in the afternoon a procession is formed in Hunnegem, the oldest quarter of the town. There are women in medieval costumes and men dressed as farmers in the time of Brueghel, and white-robed druids. As the procession reaches the Market Place, it is joined by the local dignitaries (both worldly and

spiritual), and the whole procession continues right through the town, ending up on Oudenberg Hill. Heralds bring twenty great wicker baskets full of "krakelingen" (these were originally hard, ring-shaped pretzels, but today they are round bread rolls). Other heralds carry bowls of water full of tiny live fish. A prayer is said, and then everyone gathers around the "column", the remains of an old town gate. A silver beaker of white wine teeming with fish is offered first to the dean and then the mayor. Each takes a sip, swallowing a live fish with it. Then it is the turn of the other guests. After this, the dean tosses the first krakeling to the spectators, which is a signal for the guests at

the column throw the rest of the rolls to the crowd. Everyone scrambles to catch one, because two of them contain a ticket winning the finder a handsome reward. Then the crowd sets off back down the hill to the strains of the brass band, to continue their celebrations in the town. At seven o'clock in the evening, everyone climbs up the hill again, where a barrel of flammable material has been hung up on a high mast. The mayor then sets fire to the barrel. The fiery glow of the "Tonnekensbrand" can be seen from far and wide, and it is answered by the young people in the surrounding villages as they ignite their fires in turn.

*Carnival
in Malmédy*

*The Hanswijck
Procession
in Mechelen*

FESTIVALS IN BELGIUM

Carnival	(Binche, Aalst, Malmédy, Eupen, Hasselt, Stavelot)
Dead Rat's Ball	(Ostend)
European Youth Music Festival	(Neerpelt)
Hanswijck Procession	(Mechelen)
Holy Blood Procession	(Bruges)
Procession of the Cats	(Ypres)
International Hot Air Balloon Meeting	(Ceroux-Mousty)
Traditional Shrimp Parade	(Oostduinkerke)
Hainault Flower Show	(in a different town each time)
Ommegang	(Historical pageant, in Brussels)
Rock Festival	(Torhout-Werchter)
Boat Parade - Blessing of the sea	(Ostend)
World Folklore Festival	(Schoten)
Ghent Festival	(Ghent)
Bilberry Festival and Witches' Sabbath	(Vielsalm)
Sphinx Festival	(Boechout)
Penance Procession	(Veurne)
Folk Festival	(Dranouter)
Flanders Water Festival	(Berlare)
Harvest Festival	(Rochehaut)
Internationale Dodentocht	(Bornem)
Theatre Festival	(Spa)
Patershol Festival	(Ghent)
Marktrock	(Leuven)
International Military Tattoo	(Hasselt)
International Folk Festival	(Jambes)
Grape Festival	(Overijse)
Pageant of the Golden Tree	(Bruges)
Bokrijk Festival and Rockrijk	(Genk)
Rozenberg Lantern Procession	(Mol)
Peace Festival	(Sint-Niklaas)
Walloon Festivals	(Huy, Namur, Liège)
Ivo Van Damme Memorial Event	(Brussels)
Open Monument Day	(throughout Belgium)
Brueghel Festival	(Brussels)
Festival of the Giants	(Ottignies - Louvain-La-Neuve)
Bruzzle	(Brussels)
Strip Festival	(Durbuy)
International Film Festival of Flanders	(Ghent)
Diamond Awards	(Antwerp)
Night of the Proms	(Antwerp)
ECC Tennis Tournament	(Antwerp)
Walnut Fair	(Bastogne)

HOLIDAYS

A holiday is defined as at least four consecutive nights spent away from home for recreational purposes. A short holiday (or short break) is at least one and no more than three nights spent away from home, for the same purpose. A day trip is a recreational excursion of approximately one day without an overnight stay.

In 1988, 56% of the Belgian population went on holiday: 54% in the summer (April-September) and 11% in the winter (October-March). Seventy summer holidays and 13 winter holidays are clocked up for every 100 Belgians, which is 1.48 holidays per holiday-maker. Most holiday-makers opt to stay in a hotel (31%) or rented accommodation (27%), while 13% go camping. Most travel by car (63%), 13% by plane and another 13% by coach, and 8% by train. The average length of a holiday is 14 nights (15 nights in the summer and 10 nights in the winter). The second half of July is the busiest holiday period. The average holiday party comprises 3.4 persons. One holiday in four is a seaside holiday; one holiday in ten is spent in the mountains and one in twen-

Many people today feel that a holiday is one of their rights - almost an essential part of life. Some people live for their annual holiday, and grand tours, adventure holidays and funfairs are growing more and more popular among the people.

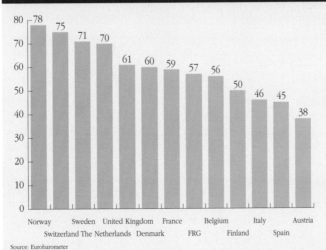

HOLIDAY PARTICIPATION IN SOME WEST EUROPEAN COUNTRIES (AROUND 1987, AS A PERCENTAGE)

Norway 78, Sweden 75, United Kingdom 71, Switzerland The Netherlands 70, France 61, Denmark 60, Belgium 59, FRG 57, Italy 56, Finland 50, Spain 46, Austria 45, 38

Source: Eurobarometer

ty is a nature, cultural or winter sports holiday.

Swedes, Norwegians and the Swiss go on holiday the most often. Significantly, they live in the countries with the highest GNP per inhabitant. The Dutch, British, Danes and French also score high in this respect, while the Belgians come fairly low in the holiday stakes.

* **In 1988, 18% of the population did not go on any kind of holiday. In Wallonia that was 30%, in the Brussels Region 14% and 12% in Flanders.**

* **The number of foreign holidays increased by 40% between 1982 and 1988.**

* **In 1987, the people of Belgium spent 8% of their total household expenditure on restaurants, cafés and hotels (excluding spending on alcohol).**

* **Almost one in three holidays are spent in a hotel.**

* **The use of the car for holidays has dropped from 69% in 1982 to 62% in 1988.**

Durbuy

HOLIDAY OPTIONS

Two thirds of all holidays in 1991 were spent outside Belgium. France, Spain and Italy were the most popular among Belgian holiday-makers.

These three countries together accounted for 60% of all holiday destinations. On the domestic front, the most popular tourist areas are the coast and the Ardennes. Almost one fifth of all holidays are spent on the coast, 8% in the Ardennes and 3% in the Kempen.

In 1991 almost one in four Belgians took a short holiday, 17% in the summer and 11% in the winter. Thirty-five short holidays were taken for every 100 inhabitants, with 22 in the summer and 13 in the winter. Just over 60% of these were spent in Belgium, mostly in a hotel. The average duration of these short breaks was 2.2 nights.

In 1991, 64% of the Belgian population went on a day-

trip. In the summer that was 58%, in the winter 26%. The average number of day trips per participant was four. Almost all day trips were to destinations inside Belgium, with the coast as the most popular choice. Towns renowned for their art, fun parks and recreation domains also attracted many visitors.

Breakdown of the Belgian holiday and recreation market in 1988:
- 62% of the population took one or more holidays or short breaks, plus day trips in some cases;
- 20% took day trips only
- 18% stayed home.

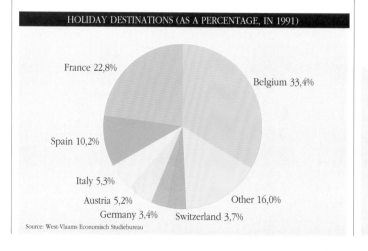

HOLIDAY DESTINATIONS (AS A PERCENTAGE, IN 1991)

France 22,8%
Belgium 33,4%
Spain 10,2%
Italy 5,3%
Austria 5,2%
Other 16,0%
Germany 3,4%
Switzerland 3,7%

Source: West-Vlaams Economisch Studiebureau

WINTER HOLIDAYS

In 1991, 15% of the Belgian population took a long holiday and 11% a short holiday in the winter. Fifteen percent of all holidays were taken in the winter. Over the last decade, the proportion of winter holidays has increased sharply. Approximately 18% of the Belgian population own mountain walking boots, 7% have ski boots, 4% alpine skis and 3% cross-country skis. Winter holidays are taken most frequently by younger people and those in the higher income groups and the professions.

TOURISM

*Tourism is booming
in Belgium.*

Tourism showed 5% growth in 1988, 11% growth in 1989 and 2% in 1990. Nights spent by tourists in Belgium rose from 30.6 million in 1984 to 36.8 million in 1990, 72% of which were in Flanders, 20% in Wallonia and 8% in Brussels. Belgian tourists accounted for 65% of the overnight stays, and tourists from neighbouring countries 26%. Of all our foreign visitors, the Dutch are the tourist industry's best customers.

The balance of tourist trade shows that every year the people of Belgium spend more on foreign travel than foreign tourists spend in Belgium. Nevertheless, earnings from tourism make a substantial contribution to state finances. In 1990, foreign

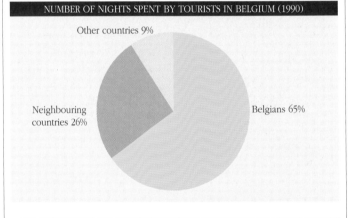

NUMBER OF NIGHTS SPENT BY TOURISTS IN BELGIUM (1990)

Other countries 9%

Neighbouring countries 26%

Belgians 65%

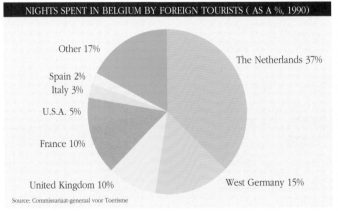

NIGHTS SPENT IN BELGIUM BY FOREIGN TOURISTS (AS A %, 1990)

Other 17%

Spain 2%
Italy 3%

U.S.A. 5%

France 10%

United Kingdom 10%

The Netherlands 37%

West Germany 15%

Source: Commissariaat-generaal voor Toerisme

tourists spent 123.4 billion BF in our country. Add to this the amount spent by the Belgians themselves on holidays and day trips in their own country, and we arrive at a total expenditure of about 160 billion BF.

Two trends can be observed regarding employment in tourism: the number of independent operators in the sector is declining (from 64 000 in 1969 to 44 000 in 1990), while the number of people employed in catering, travel agencies and local authority tourist and recreation services is increasing (from 37 000 in 1969 to 133 000 in 1990). In other words, there is a trend towards larger-scale operations.

*Spectators at the
Golden Tree
Procession
in Bruges*

TOURIST AREAS

The two most popular tourist areas in Belgium are the coast and the Ardennes.

The coast is one long beach stretching for 65 km, taking in 15 seaside towns, each with its own individual character. Its sandy beaches are the ideal children's playground. The beaches never shelve suddenly into deep sea, and lifeguards watch over bathers as they play in the shallow waters. Sunbathers will find what they want too: the iodine and salt of the Belgian coast will help you to tan faster here than in southern Europe !

The Ardennes, in south-east Belgium, are a region of unspoilt nature with extensive deciduous woods and pine forests, hills and valleys and wild rivers. The area has a rich variety of flora and fauna. Picturesque villages nestle in the valleys, where tradition and folklore are still alive.

Belgium is an ideal country for day excursions. A visit to one of the historical towns is a delightful way of learning something of the history of our country. For tourists who prefer to be out in the countryside, there is a wide range of nature reserves, zoos and recreation parks.

In 1990, the coast accounted for 44% of the nights spent by tourists in Belgium, the Ardennes 16%, the Kempen 15% and the art towns (Antwerp, Bruges, Brussels, Ghent, Leuven, Liège, Mechelen, Tournai and Tongeren) 15%.

---

* **Foreign tourists account for 92% of the nights spent by tourists in the art towns (1990).**

---

* **The coast accounts for almost half of all nights spent by tourists in Belgium (1990).**

---

* **60% of the nights are spent in hotels and camp sites (1990).**

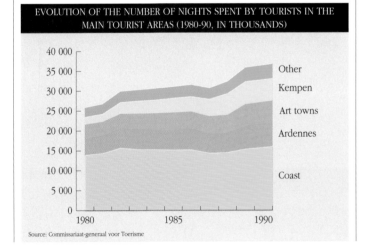

EVOLUTION OF THE NUMBER OF NIGHTS SPENT BY TOURISTS IN THE MAIN TOURIST AREAS (1980-90, IN THOUSANDS)

Other
Kempen
Art towns
Ardennes
Coast

40 000
35 000
30 000
25 000
20 000
15 000
10 000
5 000
0

1980   1985   1990

Source: Commissariaat-generaal voor Toerisme

Kayaking in the Ardennes

Sand yacht on the sandy expanse of the beach

SPORT

In 1969, only about half of the male population (53%) had ever played a sport; in 1989 that had risen to 72%. Participation in sport among the over-thirties has also increased: from 19% in 1969 to 55% in 1989.

The sharpest increase came between 1970-80, sparked off by the many sport promotion campaigns set up during that period under the "sport for everyone" policy. More women are also taking part in sport. In 1969, 25% of women in Belgium had ever played a sport, and in 1989 that figure had risen to 56%. Participation in sport after the age of thirty increased over the same period from 9% to 43%, also showing the sharpest upswing between 1970 and 1980.

Swimming pool in the Residence Palace in Brussels

* **Among men over thirty, swimming was the most popular sport in** 1969 and 1979; today it is football. Tennis is also growing in popularity.

* Among women over thirty, swimming, gym, cycling, walking and tennis are the most popular sports.

* Approximately 34% of Belgian adults are seriously interested in sport. The EUR12 average is 31% (1987).

* Almost three Flemings out of four watch the sports news on the television.

* One in five Belgians belong to a sports club.

INTEREST IN SPORT

Nine out of ten Belgians claim to have been interested in sport at some time.

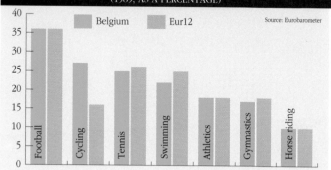

WHICH OF THESE SPORTS ARE YOU SERIOUSLY INTERESTED IN?
(1989, AS A PERCENTAGE)

Belgium   Eur12   Source: Eurobarometer

Football | Cycling | Tennis | Swimming | Athletics | Gymnastics | Horse riding

Sports programmes on the radio and television are very popular and both attract high ratings. Football leads the field in this respect. Television coverage of the World Cup in Mexico and Italy had hundreds of thousands of viewers glued to the screen, and for many matches the viewing figures topped 25%. There is always overwhelming interest in the matches played by the Belgian national team, the Red Devils.

CYCLING

*Cycling is very popular
in Belgium.
The "Flandriens" have made
history in the Tour de France,
and top cyclist Eddy Merckx
is a national hero.
Every important cycling race is
broadcast directly on radio
and television.
Amateur cycling is also very
popular among ordinary people.
On Sunday mornings, local
cycling clubs are out in force
on the roads of Belgium.*

THE PRESS

Today (1992),
28 different daily newspapers
are published in Belgium:
12 in Dutch,
15 in French and 1 in German.

That is 24 titles fewer than in 1945. The titles that have survived today belong to 10 newspaper groups. In 1945 there were 43 groups controlling 53 titles; ownership is therefore concentrated in fewer hands today. Heavy political and financial pressure often plays a decisive role in takeover battles for daily papers. The Belgian daily papers have moved from private family ownership to ownership by public companies. The two largest groups are the Vlaamse Uitgevers Maatschappij, which has 32% of the Dutch language market, and Rossel n.v. with 54% of the French language market.

In 1992, the total daily print run of all daily papers together amounted to about 1 978 000 copies, 61% of which were Dutch language papers, 38% French language and 0.6% German language papers. Approximately 85% of the Belgian population reads a newspa-

per at least occasionally, and just over half of the population older than 15 does so every day, men more than women.

Over the two decades between 1970 and 1992, the total Belgian daily paper print run dropped by about 22%; the French language papers were 41% down, German language papers 10% down and the Dutch language papers maintained the same level of sales. This

downturn was caused to a certain extent by a general tightening of the belt in many families, and also by increasing competition from other media - radio and television in particular. To combat their dwindling readership, newspaper editors have been changing both the form and the content of existing titles over recent years. Some papers gave their layout a radical facelift in an attempt to rejuvenate their circulation.

Others have introduced colour pictures, or a handier format or include special supplements (eg. sport, or local news).

Traditionally, the Belgian daily papers have clear political allegiances, but are not controlled by any political party. The various daily papers also show broad similarities.

The Belgian press also publishes a wide range of periodicals offering everything from pure facts to considered opinions, from parish magazines to specialist scientific journals, children's comics and women's magazines. Together these amount to some 8 000 titles.

---

* **Belgians spend an average of 34 minutes reading the paper.**

* **One Belgian in two over the age of 15 reads a paper every day.**

BROADCASTING

Radio and television broadcasting has developed enormously over the last three decades, evolving into an important provider of information, education and entertainment with a profound influence on the lifestyles of the people.

Belgium's geographical location in the heart of Europe has been a great stimulus for the development of communications throughout the country. In the electronics world, Belgian telephone technology enjoys international renown. The first television pictures were beamed into Belgian living rooms 35 years ago. In 1990 there were 3 300 000 TV sets in Belgium: one for every three inhabitants. With 95% of the country served by cable distribution, Belgium has the highest density cable network in the world.

Radio started out as a private initiative. The first ra-dio stations were set up in the nineteen-twenties. In the thirties a public broadcasting authority was set up which enjoyed a virtual monopoly and was only required to grant a limited amount of broadcasting time to the so-called broadcasting associations. The new broadcasting law of 18 May 1960 was a minor revolution. The greater autonomy of the new broadcasting organisations (now the BRTN and RTBF) was an important achievement. Prior government censorship was now no longer possible. The new broadcasting institutions were given a threefold task: the provision of information, education and entertainment.

In the course of the eighties, new decrees were enacted governing private radio and television. Belgium has a great number of commercial radio stations, main-ly broadcasting locally. The launching of the commercial television channels VTM and RTL-TVi at the end of the eighties was an event which was to have far-reaching consequences, and succeeded in turning the television world upside down.

---

* **The average time spent watching television rose between 1980-90 from just under 2 hours a day to 2 hours 15 minutes; average time spent listening to the radio rose from two and a half hours to three and a half hours.**

---

* **23% of families have at least two TV sets.**

THE BELGIAN MEDIA LANDSCAPE

There are six national and semi-national television channels in Belgium: three Dutch language and three French. Both Flanders and Wallonia have two public broadcasting television channels and one commercial.

There are also a number of regional television corporations. Today, early 1992, radio broadcasting has nine national and semi-national public broadcasting networks (four Dutch language, four French and one German), plus hundreds of local stations financed mainly or wholly by advertising.

There are three public broadcasting corporations: the BRTN (Dutch language broadcasting), the RTBF (French language) and the BRF (German language). These corporations operate according to the rules drawn up by the Community Councils, based on the principles of cultural autonomy, pluralism, freedom of information and unbiased news reporting. The broadcasting corporations each have their own operating budgets.

Flanders has two television channels controlled by the public broadcasting corporation the BRTN. Its French language opposite number, the RTBF, also has two television channels. At the end of the nineteen-eighties, they were joined by the domestic commercial chan-

nels: the VTM for Flanders, which was launched on 1 February 1989, and for French speaking viewers the RTL-TVi which went on the air on 5 June 1987 as a subsidiary of the RTL in Luxembourg. VTM programmes are broadcast exclusively over the cable network in Flanders and Brussels, with no aerial transmission. RTL-TVi programmes are broadcast over the cable and by aerial transmission from Luxembourg.

In Flanders, there is a clear division between public broadcasting (BRTN) and commercial broadcasting (VTM). The BRTN is allowed to broadcast commercial advertising on the radio, but not on the television. VTM has a monopoly of television advertising. In Wallonia there is no such division, and the RTBF public broadcasting corporation carries advertising on both radio and television. The RTBF and the commercial

RTL-TVi even have a common company to deal with their advertising business.

In Flanders, the new commercial broadcasting corporation VTM soon ousted the BRT from its position as market leader. With only one television channel, the VTM has higher viewing ratings than the BRTN with two channels. And it is not only the BRTN which has seen its ratings slump: Dutch channels have also felt the pinch as many of their viewers defected to VTM. Today, in 1992, VTM ratings have already risen to 40 - 45%.

There is a similar picture in Wallonia, where the public broadcasting corporation has been upstaged by the commercial RTL-TVi. And both public and commercial broadcasting in Wallonia also faces strong competition from abroad in the shape of the French commercial channel TF1, Antenne 2, Fr 3.

The German speaking region of Belgium has its own autonomous broadcasting corporation for radio, but not for television.

CHAPTER

4

LIVING IN DEMOCRACY

King Albert II taking the constitutional oath of succession before the both Chambers of Parliament on 9 August 1993.

A CONSTITU-TIONAL MONARCHY

Belgium became an independent state in 1830. On 7 February 1831 a new Constitution was proclaimed which has since been used as a model for the constitution of many countries after it.

It includes an article which states that all powers stem from the nation, i.e. the people as a whole. This is the basis of democracy in Belgium. This same constitution includes provisions governing the vestment of legislative, executive and judiciary powers.

Belgium is a hereditary monarchy. The present Head of State is King Albert II, the sixth King of the Belgians. The king enjoys personal inviolability, and his ministers are responsible for his acts. This means that no political act initiated by the king can be implemented unless it is supported by a minister. This provision places the king above religious sects, political movements and economic and social interests.

Public opinion is fairly favourable towards the monarchy. A large proportion of the population is convinced that the monarchy is a useful institution. An opinion poll carried out in 1990 by the Political Science Department of the Catholic University of Leuven revealed that six out of every ten Belgians over the age of 18 are of the opinion that Belgium needs a king. Men and women agree broadly on this, but there were differences between the age groups: the higher the age, the greater the preponderance of pro-monarchists. Wallonia has the lowest percentage of monarchists (60%), followed by Flanders (62%) and Brussels (63%). One fifth of the population considers that Belgium would be better off without a king. One third favours extending the powers of the king, and one in ten would prefer to curtail them.

In 1990 it was forty years ago that King Boudewijn succeeded his father as Prince Royal. The 7th of September was his 60th birthday, and the 40th anniversary of his accession to the throne was celebrated on 17 July 1991. This sparked off a series of festive and cultural events. The king had expressed a desire for these festivities to focus on two themes: the future of young people today and the dialogue between the communities and regions and the people.

King Boudewijn and Queen Fabiola at a children's party

A PARLIAMENTARY DEMOCRACY

Belgium is a parliamentary democracy. The constitution provides for a division of power between the legislature, executive and judiciary.

Over the years, the executive and the government in particular have grown more and more important. The so-called de facto powers such as the political parties and the partners in the social dialogue (trades unions and employers' associations) also play a leading role in political life.

Parliament

---

* **Voting is compulsory in Belgium. In answer to the question "Would you still vote if it were no longer compulsory?", 56% said that they would vote in borough council elections, 47% would do so in parliamentary elections and 45% in the elections for the European Parliament (1990).**

---

* **Since World War II, 31 elections have been held (including a referendum on the Royal Question and European and Borough Council elections).**

THE LEGISLATURE

*The most important
task of the legislature
is legislation.
Legislative power is vested
jointly in the King,
the House of Representatives
and the Senate.*

The House of Representatives has 150 members, who are elected by direct, secret vote. Suffrage in Belgium is on a one man, one vote basis: every Belgian national, male or female, who has reached the age of 18 has the right to cast one vote, unless this right has been suspended or the individual is ineligible for any reason. Everyone is obliged to take part in the elections. To be elected as a member of parliament, candidates must be Belgian, hold full civil and political rights, be domiciled in Belgium and at least 21 years of age.

The Senate is composed of 71 members.

There are four categories of senators:
– 40 senators elected by direct suffrage; 25 of these are chosen by Dutch-speaking electors and 15 by French-speakers;
– 21 senators elected by the Community Councils (Community senators); 10 of these senators represent the Flemish Community, 10 the French-speaking Commu-

nity and 1 the German-speaking Community;
– 10 co-opted senators; they are elected by the directly elected senators and the Community senators. Six of them represent the Dutch-speaking Community and four the French-speaking Community;
– Senators "by right". These are the children of the King, or if there are none, the

descendants of the ruling branch of the royal family, if they are of Belgian nationality and over 18 years of age. They have a vote from the age of 21.

The Chamber of Representatives and the Senate enjoy equal powers regarding amendments to the Constitution and a number of important laws, which means that they must both pass the same texts. With respect to other legislation, the Senate has only a right to initiate, and a right to have a say of some kind. The Chamber alone bears responsibility for other matters, including the control of the government, the budgets, and naturalization.

*The House of
Representatives*

THE EXECUTIVE AND THE LEGISLATURE

The task of the executive is the execution of the law.

Executive power is vested in the king and the ministers, and is exercised mainly through Royal and Ministerial Decrees. References in the constitution to the power vested in the king, always mean the power the king exercises jointly with his ministers. At national level, executive power is wielded in practice by the government.

The judiciary settles disputes arising in the application of the law. Judges enjoy constitutional guarantees such as appointment for life which are intended to promote their independence. In addition to the ordinary law courts, the most important of which are the civil and criminal courts, there are also administrative courts with the Council of State as the highest. For ordinary law, the Court of Cassation is the supreme court. The Court of Arbitration is responsible for ensuring that the legislation of the Communities and the Regions respects the distribution of powers and also certain rights and freedoms to which the Belgian people are entitled.

---

* **Since the end of World War II, Belgium has already had 36 different governments.**

FLAGS & FESTIVALS

The heraldic emblem of Belgium is the lion (Leo Belgicus) with the motto: "Eendracht maakt macht" (strength lies in unity). The national anthem is the "Brabançonne".

The colours of the Belgian flag are black, yellow and red, in vertical stripes. The national festival is celebrated on 21 July, the anniversary of the day on which Leopold I took the oath as the first King of the Belgians in 1831. The "Day of the Dynasty" is celebrated on 15 November.

There are also other official flags apart from the national tricolour. The flag of the Flemish Community bears a black lion with red claws and tongue against a yellow background. The feast day of the Flemish Community is celebrated on 11 July, the anniversary of the Battle of the Golden Spurs (1302), in which Gewijde van Dampierre, Count of Flanders, and the borough militia

were victorious over the King of France and his allies.

The French Community has a red cockerel as its emblem, and their flag shows a red cockerel against a yellow background. The feast day of the French Community is on 27 September, commemorating the victory of the patriots over the Dutch in the Park of Brussels in 1830.

The flag of the German speaking Community is a red lion surrounded by nine blue cinquefoils against a white background. The feast day of the German speaking Community is on 15 November, which is also the Day of the Dynasty.

POLY-LINGUALISM

*Geographically,
Belgium lies on the dividing line
between the Latin
and Germanic cultures.
This in itself largely explains
the Belgian
linguistic situation.*

Belgium has three official languages: Dutch, French and German. Two large population groups live side by side: the Dutch speaking Flemish Community in Flanders, in the north, and the French speaking Community in Wallonia in the south. Brussels is bilingual, with the French speakers in the majority. Belgium is divided by the language frontier which runs from east to west. There is also a German speaking Community in the eastern corner of the province of Liège, as a result of the acquisition of a number of German cantons

after the first world war. On the basis of these linguistic and other differences, Belgium could lay claim, up to a point, to three different cultures. The well-known Flemish saying "De tael is gansch het volk" (language sums up the people) dates from 1834. This cultural diversity brings both enrichment and conflict. Over the last few decades, it has led to fundamental constitutional reforms resulting in a quasi-federal structure based on the constitutional recognition of the three Communities and the three Regions.

The presence of two large communities in Belgium has left its mark on all aspects of life. In the Cabinet, the main organ of national executive power, there must be equal numbers of Dutch speaking and French speaking ministers, with the possible exception of the prime minister. That is also the case in the Brussels-Capital Region Executive. In the Court of Arbitration, the Court of Cassation and the Council of State (the highest organs of judicial power), there must be equal numbers of French speaking and Dutch speaking judges.

In the central departments of state administration dealing with the country as a whole, and in local administration in the bilingual region of Brussels-Capital, posts above a certain level must be divided equally between employees in the French speaking service and those in the Dutch speaking service. Similar provisions govern appointments in the services of the Brussels-Capital Region Executive.

This provided that in monolingual regions, the use of the language of the region was compulsory for all public administrative acts. The language laws of 1962 divided the country into four linguistic regions: three monolingual linguistic regions (the Dutch speaking, French speaking and German speaking regions) and one bilingual region, Brussels-Capital (Greater Brussels). This division of Belgium was enshrined in the Constitution of 1970. The Dutch speaking Region comprises the five Flemish provinces: Antwerp, Limburg, East Flanders, West Flanders plus Flemish Brabant (the administrative districts of Leuven and Halle-Vilvoorde). The French speaking Region comprises the five Walloon provinces: Hainault, Luxembourg, Namur, Liège (with the exception of the boroughs belonging to the German speaking Region) plus Walloon Brabant (the administrative district of Nivelles). The German speaking Region comprises 9 boroughs in the eastern part of the province of Liège. The bilingual Brussels-Capital Region comprises the 19 boroughs of the metropolitan administrative area of Greater Brussels, including the city of Brussels.

In Belgium, every effort is made to protect minorities from discrimination. In the first reform of the state in

A COMPLEX STATE STRUCTURE

*The language laws
of 1962-63
laid the foundations
of the "territoriality principle".*

1970, a number of protective measures were introduced. One of these was the special majority law, defined as an act of Parliament passed on majority vote in each linguistic group in each of the Houses of Parliament, on condition that the majority of the members of each group are present and that total votes in favour in each Chamber attain two thirds of the votes cast. This is generally known as the "limitation procedure" or community majority law. The purpose of this stringent requirement was to prevent the growth of a body of fundamental laws governing the structure of the state against the wishes of either of the country's two main Communities. A further measure was the introduction of the alarm-bell procedure. The "alarm-bell" is sounded by a reasoned motion signed by at least three quarters of the members of one of the linguistic groups. This procedure is designed to prevent the adoption by majority vote of a single linguistic group (chiefly the Dutch linguistic group, which holds a majority in both chambers) of any legislation which could have a serious effect on the relations between the two (major) Communities. Sounding the alarm bell results in the suspension of parliamentary procedure. The Cabinet must then give its reasoned findings on the motion and invite the House before which it was tabled to reach a decision either on those findings or on the bill, amended as may be. This is primarily a preventive measure, since the Cabinet, comprising equal numbers of each linguistic group, will endeavour to reach a consensus solution on the problem and thus avert a government crisis. An ideological alarm-bell procedure also operates within each Community Council. Finally, since 1970, the development of the Brussels-Capital Regional institutions has incorporated various safeguards for the protection of the Dutch speaking minority.

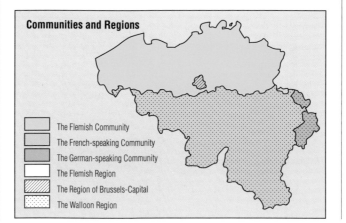

Communities and Regions

- The Flemish Community
- The French-speaking Community
- The German-speaking Community
- The Flemish Region
- The Region of Brussels-Capital
- The Walloon Region

The "Botanique" in Brussels, the cultural centre of the French speaking Community

COMMUNITIES & REGIONS

In Belgium, a distinction is made between Communities and Regions.

The formation of the Communities met one of the long-standing demands of the Flemish Movement, which had always fought for full recognition and development of its language and culture. In 1970, three cultural communities were recognised in the constitution, namely the Dutch, French and German speaking cultural communities. Each was equipped with its own institutions vested with powers to enact decrees with legislative force for the territories under their authority in matters relating to cultural affairs and (to a more limited extent) education and the use of languages. The 1980 Constitutional revision turned cultural autonomy into Community autonomy following the extension of their powers to cover "personalized" matters, and the creation of their own executive bodies. In the 1988 revision of the Constitution, the autonomy of the Communities was further strengthened by the assignation of virtually full responsibility for education to the Communities, and even the power to conclude treaties in matters falling within their competence.

The 1993 Constitutional revision (implementing the Sint-Michiels agreement) completed the federal state structure by the introduction of measures such as the direct election of the legislative bodies of Communities and Regions and the banning of the so-called "double mandate", the reform of Chamber and Senate, the division of the province of Brabant and a further extension of the powers of Communities and Regions (including full power to conclude treaties).

If the formation of the Communities was principally a Flemish initiative, the formation of the Regions was initiated by the Franco-phones. The Walloons hoped to solve their economic crisis through autonomy over social and economic affairs, and the French speaking inhabitants of Brussels militated for the Brussels-Capital region to be recognised as a Region in its own right. This culminated in the Constitutional revision of 1970 recognising three Regions: the Flemish Region, the Walloon Region and the Brussels Region. No legislative authority was vested in the Regions in the 1970 Constitution. Since Belgian public law provides that legislative authority can be exercised only by bodies invested with that power by the Constitution, a new constitutional provision was enacted in 1980 enabling the power to make decrees to be conferred on the regional bodies by a special-majority law. That was subsequently done for the Flemish Region and the Walloon Region, but not to the same extent for the Brussels-Capital Region, which was given the power to make "ordinances" - a new legal norm in Belgian public law. Like the decree, an ordinance may repeal, amplify, amend or replace prevailing legislative provisions and is subject to the same judicial control by the Court of Arbitration. But unlike decrees, ordinances are subject to limited judicial review as well as, in certain cases, limited administrative control by the national authorities "to protect Brussels' international role and its function as the capital".

The three Communities (the Dutch speaking, French speaking and German speaking Communities) also enjoy autonomy in the regional aspects of cultural, linguistic and "personalized" matters (i.e. matters concerning personal life), and domestic and international cultural cooperation. That means that the French and Dutch speaking Communities work together to a certain extent in the Brussels Region.

The three Regions (Flemish Region, Walloon Region and Brussels Region) have competence over regional aspects of matters concerning the environment, housing, water policy, economic policy, energy, employment, public works and transport. The administrative tutelage over the provinces and boroughs also falls under the competence of the Regions.

Each Community or Region has a Council (a parliamentary assembly) and a Government.
– The Council of the Brussels-Capital Region consists of 75 directly elected members, who are divided into a Dutch language group and a French language group.
– The Flemish Council, which is in a sense the Flemish Community and the Flemish Region rolled into one, is composed of 118 directly elected members from the Flemish Region plus 6 members elected from the Dutch language

group of the Brussels-Capital Council (= a total of 124 members).
– The Council of the Walloon Region has 75 directly elected members.
– The Council of the French Community is composed of the 75 members of the Walloon Region Council plus 19 members elected from and by the French language group of the Brussels-Capital Council.
– 25 directly elected members sit on the Council of the German speaking Community.

The executive organs of the Communities and the Regions are the Flemish Government (max. 11 members), the French Community Government (max. 4 members), the Walloon Region Government (max. 7 members), the Brussels-Capital Government (5 members) and the Government of the German speaking Community (3 members).

On certain conditions, the Flemish Council, the Council of the Walloon Region

and the Council of the French Community may alter the number of members of their own Council or Government, by means of a decree which must be passed by a majority of two-thirds.

---

* **In 1989, the financial resources of the Communities together amounted to 388 billion BF; the Regions' resources totalled 261 billion BF. This represents 40% of state expenditure, excluding interest.**

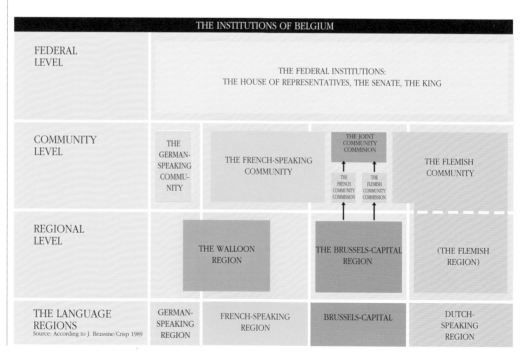

THE INSTITUTIONS OF BELGIUM				
FEDERAL LEVEL	THE FEDERAL INSTITUTIONS: THE HOUSE OF REPRESENTATIVES, THE SENATE, THE KING			
COMMUNITY LEVEL	THE GERMAN-SPEAKING COMMU-NITY	THE FRENCH-SPEAKING COMMUNITY	THE JOINT COMMUNITY COMMISION / THE FRENCH COMMUNITY COMMISSION / THE FLEMISH COMMUNITY COMMISSION	THE FLEMISH COMMUNITY
REGIONAL LEVEL		THE WALLOON REGION	THE BRUSSELS-CAPITAL REGION	(THE FLEMISH REGION)
THE LANGUAGE REGIONS Source: According to J. Brassine/Crisp 1989	GERMAN-SPEAKING REGION	FRENCH-SPEAKING REGION	BRUSSELS-CAPITAL	DUTCH-SPEAKING REGION

PROVINCES & BOROUGHS

The provinces and boroughs are territorial constituents of the state. They are also autonomous political bodies to whom competence has been devolved for certain matters. Their administrative structure is defined by law, and they act under government supervision.

The Flemish Region is divided into the provinces of Antwerp, Limburg, East Flanders, Flemish Brabant and West Flanders. The Walloon Region comprises the provinces of Hainault, Liège, Luxembourg, Namur and Walloon Brabant. The bilingual Brussels-Capital Region does not constitute a province, but its institutions have been assigned most of the powers of a province. The people of each province are represented in a Provincial Council whose members are elected directly for six years by all electors of the province, at the same time as the Municipal Council elections. Competences are vested in the Provincial Council regarding the general running of the nation, in addition to their basic competence to deal with all matters of provincial interest in general. An Executive Committee comprising six members is nominated within the Provincial Council. This Committee is charged with the day-to-day management and the execution of council decisions. The state is represented in

each province by a Governor, who is appointed by the King and responsible for overseeing the correct execution of laws, decrees and decisions in the province. He is a co administrator of the province as chairman (and voting member) of the Executive Committee.

Up to 1977, Belgium had over 2 500 municipalities or boroughs. In that year radical mergers brought the number of boroughs down to 589. The autonomy of the borough is something

dear to the hearts of most Belgians, and many feel a personal involvement in the actions and policies of their borough. The representative assembly of the borough is the Borough Council, whose members are elected every six years by the electors of the borough. The number of members sitting on the Borough Council is proportional to the number of inhabitants in the borough. The Borough Council must have at least seven members (including the Mayor and Al-

dermen) in boroughs with under 1 000 inhabitants and no more than 55 members in boroughs of over 300 000 inhabitants. All borough matters, including the budget, bills and taxes, are dealt with in the Borough Council. The decisions of the Borough Council are implemented by the Mayor and Aldermen. The Mayor is appointed by the king, on the recommendation of the Borough Council, which also nominates the Aldermen. The Mayor is the representative of the government in the borough.

* **The total number of seats in the Provincial Councils is 716. In the Provincial Councils of Antwerp, Brabant, Hainault, East Flanders and West Flanders there are 90 seats, 86 in Liège, 70 in Limburg, 60 in Namur and 50 in Luxembourg.**

* **Since 1988, there are a total of 12 751 Borough Councillors in Belgium, which is equal to 0.17% of the population aged 18 or over.**

*The Belfry,
symbol of
municipal
freedom,
in Bruges*

INTEREST IN POLITICS

The average Belgian has little interest in politics. According to a European poll, fewer than one in ten Belgians are keenly interested in politics, and six out of ten say they are not very interested or not interested at all.

There is also little enthusiasm for concrete political action. As far as conventional political action is concerned (i.e. following politics with interest in the media and militant political participation), according to a poll taken in 1990, nine out of ten Belgians had participated in no more than three types of conventional political action. And this political action was no more than following the political news passively through the media and political discussions. In every Region, four out of every ten took part in no conventional political action whatsoever.

More involvement was shown in the field of non-conventional political action

(i.e. concrete political protest, such as signing a petition, taking part in a peaceful demonstration, striking or cooperating in a boycot). Four out of ten Belgians say they take part in a number of types of non-conventional political action: 43% in Brussels, 39% in Flanders and 34% in Wallonia. Approximately one in three take part in no non-conventional political action, or only one type.

---

* **62% of the Belgian population has little interest in politics, or no interest at all.**

---

* **One Belgian in five is interested in international politics (Eur 12 = 17%).**

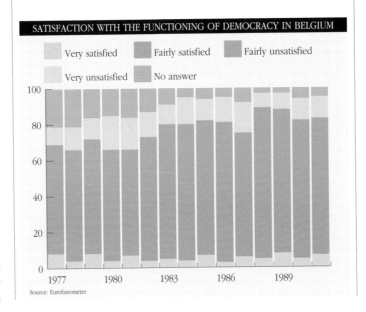

SATISFACTION WITH THE FUNCTIONING OF DEMOCRACY IN BELGIUM

Very satisfied   Fairly satisfied   Fairly unsatisfied

Very unsatisfied   No answer

1977   1980   1983   1986   1989

Source: Eurobarometer

POLITICAL LOYALTY

In 1987, a poll was carried out among 1000 sixth-formers in Flanders to measure their national awareness. They were asked how much of a bond they felt with their borough, province, Flanders, Belgium and Europe.

By far the strongest bond was with the borough: six out of ten sixth-formers felt they belonged to their own home town first and foremost. Next, after a wide gap, came Flanders (17%), then Belgium (11%), Europe (8%) and finally their own province (5%). The bond became more tenuous the more distant the geographical entity was. This trend is most visible at the extremes: a large majority feels the closest bond with their home borough, and an almost equal number the loosest bond with Europe. In other words, young people in Flanders have a somewhat parochial focus, and feel little supranational involvement. There is no feeling of national awareness or patriotism.

In a poll carried out in 1990 by the Department of Political Science of the Catholic University of Leuven, a representative sam-

BOND (FIRST CHOICE) WITH ONE'S HOME BOROUGH, FLANDERS, WALLONIA, BELGIUM OR EUROPE (AS A %, 1991, BELGIAN POPULATION)			
	Flanders	Wallonia	Brussels
Borough	49.9	28.6	28.6
Flanders	22.0	-	4.1
Wallonia	-	22.7	5.8
Belgium	18.5	30.3	32.3
Europe	9.6	18.4	29.3

Source: Department of Political Science, Catholic University of Leuven.

ple of the Belgian population (1 000 Flemings, 1 000 Walloons and 1 000 inhabitants of Brussels, all 18 years old or over) answered questions about the strength of the bond they felt with their own home borough, Flanders, Wallonia, Belgium and Europe. For Flanders and Wallonia there were four possible choices, and five for Brussels. One out of two in Flanders gave their own home borough as first choice, followed by Flanders in second place, and then Belgium. Only one Fleming in ten gave Europe as first choice. In Wallonia and Brussels there was a different picture: there, almost one in three replies gave Belgium as first choice, and then their home borough. For Walloons, Wallonia only rates third place. In Brussels, almost one in three replies gave Europe as first choice.

THE POLITICAL PARTIES

Political preferences emerge clearly at election time, and the political parties play a key role here.

It is the political parties that determine the character of the political landscape. Although there is no mention of political parties in the Constitution, in practice they play a powerful role. In a sense, they stand between the electorate and their representatives; it is the political parties who decide the order of the candidates and present them to the electorate. The Legislative Assemblies also recognise the reality of the power of the political parties, and provide for the formation of parliamentary groups which in fact represent the parties.

The Liberal Party was the first political party in Belgium. It was founded in 1846, and in 1961 became the Partij voor Vrijheid en Vooruitgang (Party for Freedom and Progress). Since 1971, it has had two branches: the PVV (Flemish liberals) and the PRL (Parti Réformateur Libéral - the Walloon liberals).

The second political group is the Catholic party, which was founded in 1884, and became the Christelijke Volkspartij (Christian People's Party - christian democrats) in 1945. In 1968 it split into two autonomous branches which were later set up as autonomous parties in their own right: the Christelijke Volkspartij (CVP) in Flanders and the Parti Social Chrétien (PSC) in Wallonia.

In 1885 a socialist party was set up: the Belgische Werkliedenpartij (Belgian Workers' Party), which functioned clandestinely during the war, and was dissolved in 1940. In 1945 the Belgische Socialistische Partij (Belgian Socialist Party - BSP) was created to take its place. A split came in 1978 between the Dutch speaking members and the Francophones, and today there are two independent parties: the Flemish Socialistische Partij and the Walloon Parti Socialiste.

There are (or have been) other smaller parties too: the Communist Party (KPB/PCB), the Partij van de Arbeid (formerly AMADA) (Labour Party), the Revolutionaire Arbeidersliga (Revolutionary Workers' Party - RAL), Respect voor Arbeid en Democratie (RAD, UDRT) and Solidarité et Participation (SEP).

In Flanders there is also the Volksunie (VU), a Flemish nationalist party. The Rassemblement Wallon (RW), its opposite number in Wallonia, has disappeared from the political scene. Support for the Front des Francophones (FDF) is confined mainly to Brussels. The right-wing Flemish nationalist party Vlaams Blok has also figured in the elections since 1978.

There has been growing support for the Greens in Belgium since the late seventies: AGALEV in Flanders and ECOLO in Wallonia.

---

* Approximately 6% of the Belgians claim to belong to a political party or movement (EUR12 = 5%).

VOTING

Over the years, the percentage of votes (and seats) won by the major political groupings has changed substantially.

After World War II, the Catholic family of parties' share of the votes peaked at 48% in 1950. In terms of seats, this meant that the Christelijke Volkspartij then had an absolute majority with 108 of the 212 seats. Support for the CVP/PSC was at its lowest ebb in 1981, when it netted only 27% of the votes (61 seats). The socialists have between 25% (1981) and 37% (1954) of the votes, and liberals between 22% (1965 and 1981) and 9% (1946).

Between 1961 and 1971, the three traditional parties (christian democrats, socialists and liberals) faced a particularly strong challenge from the success of the regional parties (the Volksunie in Flanders, Rassemblement Wallon in Wallonia, Front des Francophones in Brussels). In 1961, the three large political families had over 90% of the votes (House of Representatives); in 1971 that had fallen to 74%. The Volksunie, Rassemblement Wallon and Front des Francophones together gathered up 22% of the votes in that year. From 1971 onwards, the linguistic poles of the national parties evolved into autonomous parties in their

Drawing the list numbers for an election

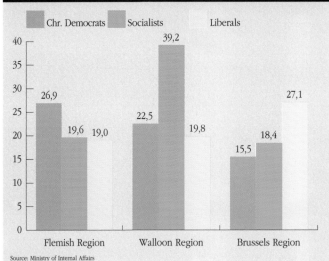

RESULTS OF THE 1991 PARLIAMENTARY ELECTIONS FOR THE THREE MAIN POLITICAL FAMILIES, PER BOROUGH (HOUSE OF REPRESENTATIVES, AS A PERCENTAGE)

Source: Ministry of Internal Affairs

own right. The growth of the christian democrats in the period up to 1978 is particularly striking. This was attributed to the reformulation of the party's christian profile, among other factors, and to the successful rejuvenation of the party image which attracted an influx of new, younger voters in the seventies.

The 1978 elections were overshadowed by intercommunity tensions. This led to the mobilisation of the Flemish militant organisations, and the establishment of a breakaway group from the Volksunie as the Vlaams Blok. The Volksunie had just been a member of the coalition government, which had displeased many Volksunie voters. Support for the Volksunie slumped, with large numbers of voters defecting to the Vlaams Blok, and other parties. From this point on, the Christelijke Volkspartij also took on a more and more pronounced community profile in Flanders, just as the Parti Socialiste in Wallonia.

The parliamentary elections of 8 November 1981 were a heavy blow for the christian democrats. The CVP/PSC won almost 450 000 fewer votes than in the previous elections, despite the fact that there were over 500 000 more electors on the roll following the lowering of the voting age to 18. The CVP/PSC lost a quarter of its voters in 1981: the largest loss since the second world war and an all-time low. In contrast, the liberals booked one of their best results. All this tended to level out the differences between the power bases of the parties. The CVP/PSC had 61 seats, the socialists the same number, and the liberals 52.

In the 1985 elections, the government parties and the main opposition party (the socialists) won more votes. The christian democrats came out with 69 seats, the socialists 67 and the liberals 46. The extra seats won by these parties was at the cost of the community based parties, the communists and a number of smaller parties. The greens won their first big success in the 1985 elections, when the number of green seats went up from 4 to 9.

The 1987 elections showed a different picture again, with the Flemish christian democrats suffering large

vote losses (2%), while the Parti Socialiste won an extra 2%. This makes the socialist family the largest parliamentary party today, with 31% of the votes and 72 of the 212 seats in the House of Representatives.

In the 1991 elections, the ruling coalition lost many votes. The Flemish christian democrats and the Flemish socialists fell back to a record low, while the Flemish liberals in the opposition booked only a modest gain. In Wallonia, the three traditional parties suffered losses. In Flanders, the

Vlaams Blok and the new "Rossem" party chalked up gains, as did Ecolo (the green party) in Wallonia. Votes for these parties are generally interpreted as protest votes.

* **The number of absentees at parliamentary elections was between 5% and 7% over the last few years, and the number of blank or spoiled ballot papers between 6% and 8%.**

* **There were approximately 50% personal preferential votes cast in**

the elections for the House of Representatives and 40% in the elections for the Senate.

* **The percentage of personal preferential votes is substantially lower among green votes than among votes for the traditional parties. In 1987 there were 24% personal preferential votes for the greens, as against 60% for the christian democrats.**

DISTRIBUTION OF SEATS IN THE HOUSE OF REPRESENTATIVES											
	CVP PSC	(B) SP PS (B)	PVV PLP/PRL	KP PC	FDF (RW)	RW	VU	PLDP	Agalev ECOLO	RAD UDRT	VL blok
1946	92	69	17	23	-	-	-	-	-	-	-
1949	105	66	29	12	-	-	-	-	-	-	-
1950	108	77	20	7	-	-	-	-	-	-	-
1954	95	86	25	4	-	-	1	-	-	-	-
1958	104	84	21	2	-	-	1	-	-	-	-
1961	96	84	20	5	-	-	5	-	-	-	-
1965	77	64	48	6	3	2	12	-	-	-	-
1968	69	59	47	5	12	-	20	-	-	-	-
1971	67	61	34	5	24	-	21	-	-	-	-
1974	72	59	30	4	22	-	22	3	-	-	-
1977	80	62	31	2	15	-	20	2	-	-	-
1978	82	58	36	4	11	4	14	1	-	-	-
1981	61	61	52	2	8	-	20	-	4	3	1
1985	69	67	46	-	3	-	16	-	9	1	1
1987	62	72	48	-	3	-	16	-	9	-	2
1991	57	63	46	-	3	-	10	-	17	-	12

Source: NIS and CRISP. The difference between the total and 212 is the number of seats won by other parties.

THE BELGIANS

The Jubelpark in Brussels

EUROPEAN AMBITIONS

*Belgium is the political
heart of Europe.
One of the reasons for this is
its central geographical location,
which has made Belgium an ideal
meeting place throughout the ages
for peoples from all corners
of the world.*

Many of the big multinationals in industry, commerce and finance have their central offices in Belgium. Brussels plays a key role here. Tens of millions of Europeans live within a radius of 400 km around the Belgian capital. This represents one of the largest consumer markets in the world. It includes cities like Antwerp, Rotterdam, Cologne, Luxembourg, Paris and London, all of which are linked by the densest communications network in the world. The choice of Brussels as the political capital of Europe confirms its function as the place where all roads meet. The activities of the European Community may be divided between Brussels, Strasbourg and Luxembourg, but the political and business centre of the Community is in Brussels. This is where all the offices are, and where the three main European institutions have their headquarters: the European Commission, the Economic and Social Committee and the European Council of Ministers.

New facilities for conferences and meetings are being built to provide an even better service for the European institutions

BRUSSELS

- IS THE CAPITAL OF BELGIUM.

- BRUSSELS IS THE FOURTH CONFERENCE CITY
  AND THE SEVENTH FINANCIAL
  CENTRE IN THE WORLD.

- IT IS THE ADMINISTRATIVE SEAT
  OF THE EC AND NATO.

- IT PARTICIPATES IN THE BIG EUROPEAN
  TECHNOLOGICAL PROJECTS LIKE
  EUREKA, ESPRIT, BRITE, EURAM,
  VERY LARGE TELESCOPE ETC..

- IT IS BUILDING A "EUROPEAN QUARTER"
  FOR THE SINGLE MARKET OF 1992.

- IT IS PLANNING A STATION FOR
  THE HIGH SPEED TRAIN, WITH CONNECTIONS
  TO GERMANY, FRANCE AND THE NETHERLANDS.

- IT WILL BE LINKED WITH THE EUROTUNNEL
  BETWEEN FRANCE AND THE UK.

- IT IS PLANNING TO EXTEND ITS
  AIRPORT FACILITIES SO THAT TWICE AS MANY
  PASSENGERS AND TWICE AS MUCH FREIGHT CAN
  BE HANDLED BY THE YEAR 2005.

The Market Place in Brussels, decorated with a flower carpet

BELGIUM AND EUROPEAN INTEGRATION

Belgium's European vocation was already clear during the war, in 1943.

Belgium signed a customs union in London with its two neighbours: the Netherlands and the Grand Duchy of Luxembourg. In 1958 this agreement was transformed into an economic union: the Benelux. At about the same time, Robert Schuman and Jean Monnet were propagating the idea of a united Europe. Belgium was immediately enthusiastic about the plan. The first step towards this united Europe was the creation of the European Coal and Steel Community (ECSC).

Belgian politicians and diplomats played an important part in the development of the European organisations. The names of Paul-Henri

Spaak and Paul van Zeeland (both of whom have been both Prime Minister and Minister of Foreign Affairs), Baron Snoy et d'Oppuers, Secretary General for Economic Affairs, Hubert Ansiaux, the Governor of the National Bank, and Roger Ockrent, Permanent Representative at the Organisation for Economic Cooperation and Development, are all closely linked with the development of Europe.

The ECSC, the first phase of economic integration, came into being thanks to the efforts of Jean Monnet, Robert Schuman and Konrad Adenauer. But it was above all through the initiative and

OPINION OF THE SINGLE EUROPEAN MARKET (1989, AS A PERCENTAGE)					
	Belgium	Netherlands	Germany	France	Eur 12
Good	58	52	46	45	55
Neither good nor bad	29	35	35	43	29
Bad	4	6	9	8	8
Don't know	8	7	11	5	9

Source: Eurobarometer

stimulation of Paul-Henri Spaak and his team (Baron Snoy et d'Oppuers, Ambassador Forthomme Rothschild and Ambassador Albert Huppers) that a desire grew to take practical steps towards setting up the European Community. Spaak worked in close cooperation with his colleague from Luxembourg Prime Minister Bech, and Minister for Foreign Affairs Beyen of the Netherlands towards achieving this. The Spaak report culminated in the signature of the Treaty of Rome by six countries on 25 March 1957, thereby founding the EEC. J. Rey of Belgium was the first chairman of the Commission of the EEC, and one of the most important architects of a united Europe.

Gradually, the conviction grew that a united Europe needed a political dimension, and once again it was a Belgian who played a leading role: viscount E. Davignon. The Davignon Report, which was approved by the European Ministers in October 1970, presented a blueprint for European political cooperation, clearing the way for harmonisation of foreign relations between the Member States.

Yet again, it was a Belgian, Prime Minister Leo Tindemans, who proposed setting up a committee of three wise men to work out a detailed plan. This was approved, but on the insistence of the British Prime Minister Harold Wilson, it was entrusted to one man instead of three. That man was Leo Tindemans. The Tindemans Report, which was published in January 1976, is still an important political document today.

---

* **Belgium has 24 seats in the European Parliament (total=518 members).**

---

* **92% are strongly in favour or very strongly in favour of European unity (EUR12=89%).**

---

* **Seven Belgians in ten consider that Belgian membership of the European Community is a good thing; only 6% are against it.**

---

* **There are 17 commissioners in the European Commission. Each of the large Member Countries provide two commissioners, and the smaller countries, including Belgium, provide one each.**

Mijn kansen staan in de sterren.

Ons Onderwijs spreekt vele talen

CHAPTER

5

WORK & PROSPERITY

POST-WAR SURVEY

Belgium made a faster recovery after the Second World War than other European countries, partly because it had suffered comparatively little war damage and partly because attempts to put the currency back on a sound basis were successful.

However, this recovery was short-lived: by the fifties, economic performance was beginning to slump. What had been an advantage after the War, later proved to be a disadvantage. Belgium was saddled with an antiquated industrial structure. Moreover, traditional heavy industries (such as coal and steel) and the textile industry were the corner-stone of Belgian industry and these sectors were coming increasingly under threat.

In the fifties and sixties, so-called mixed economies were developed. Belgium is a typical example. The system provides for cooperation between employees, employers and Government, organised on a social-economic level by all sorts of consultative bodies. The Ministry of Social Security was set up as early as September 28th 1944. It worked out schemes relating to old-age pensions, compulsory sickness insurance, invalidity and involuntary unemployment, child benefits and holiday allowances. The intention was to protect the Belgians against the vagaries of the economy. In reality, it was seen as a right to employment, a means towards increased purchasing power and the fair distribution of income. The Government had to exercise its considerable powers to implement the schemes. During this period large-scale public works programmes were begun. The law of August 9th 1955 established a Road Fund for building motorways and the law of July 5th 1956 prepared the way for large-scale development work at the Port of Antwerp. In the Brussels region major infrastructure work was carried out in connection with the 1958 World Fair. The result of all this activity was a government deficit. In 1960 the so-called "single law" came into ef-

fect, bringing tax increases and fewer subsidies.

The "silver fifties" were followed by the "golden sixties". Between 1960 and 1974 the gross national product increased by an average of 5% annually. The Planning Bureau was set up in 1959 to lead the desire for expansion and economic optimism. Wage levels rose to the highest in Europe and durable consumable goods and luxury products lay within reach of almost everyone.

But at the same time criticism of the welfare state began to grow, for not everyone benefited equally from progress. The nature of the protests became increasingly alarming, resulting, for example, in the student revolts of May '68. The media were paying more and more attention to the polluting and other negative effects of economic growth. The Report of the Club of Rome only added to the general climate of dissatisfaction. Then came the Yom Kippur War (1973). Once the OPEC countries had announced an oil embargo against Israel's allies, oil prices quadrupled within a very short space of time. The transfer of profits to the oil-producing countries diminished the purchasing power of the Western industrialised countries. The inflation rate accelerated. In 1974 price rises reached almost 16%. By linking wages to the retail price index, nominal incomes rose substantially. In fact, they rose even faster than prices.

All this led to high inflation, rising unemployment, a fall in productivity at work and a negative trade balance during the second half of the seventies. The level of unemployment increased from 4% in 1970 to 7.1% in 1978 and to 11.5% in 1981. In 1983, at the height of the crisis, the level of unemployment reached 13%. The Belgian Government fought back by creating more jobs in the public services and by giving increased help to employment programmes in the private sector. Social security payments were also extended, leading to a sharp rise in government expenditure. The interest burden on the government debt also grew, thereby reducing the margin for further government expenditure.

THE EIGHTIES

The economy seemed to be recovering slowly at the end of the seventies but war in the Gulf in 1980 resulted in a second oil crisis.

1981 saw a decline in the gross national product. Between 1974 and 1984, growth in the GNP averaged 1.3% compared with 5% in the previous decade. The general climate of malaise gradually gave rise to the view that only an effective structural economic policy would boost the economy. The voices of those economists who favoured a new producer-oriented government policy with a neo-liberal and monetary bias grew louder and louder. 1982 saw the formation of a Cabinet of Christian Democrats and Liberals which implemented this policy in which income restraint played a vital role. Its first priority was the recovery of the international competitive strength of Belgian companies. Devaluation of the Belgian franc by 8.5% in February 1982 provided the starting-shot. Major wage sacrifices and cuts in the social sector followed.

Another aspect of policy during this period was the reduction of the government deficit and the public debt. The interest payable on the debts was very high and limited government scope for implementing an active employment policy. The net amount that needed to be financed in 1982 totalled 12.4% of the gross national product. Belgium had a debt ratio which was 2.4 times larger than the OECD average. In the second phase of the recovery policy, the Government concentrated on putting government finances back on a healthy footing.

From the end of the seventies, the interest burden also began to weigh on the State's total package of debts. With the so-called Crocus Plan (1984) and the St. Anna Savings Plan (1986) the Government succeeded in pushing the deficit down to 8.1% of the gross national product in 1987 and to 7.8% in 1989. Drastic savings were realised by making changes in social security and increasing taxation. It was not long before all these measures bore fruit. After 1984, Belgium benefited from the revival in the world economic situation. There was a marked increase in exports, one of the vital strengths behind Belgian economic growth. Growth in investments (both private residential building and business investments) was among the highest in the OECD group of countries in the eighties. Inflation came down. Unemployment still remained high at first but the end of the eighties brought signs of a downward trend. Nevertheless, unemployment figures remained high.

---

* **Inflation in Belgium stood at 3.2% in 1991 (Eur12: 6%).**

---

* **In 1988 the average Belgian produced 277 kg. of household waste, compared with 110 kg. in 1950. Companies produce 10 times more waste than households.**

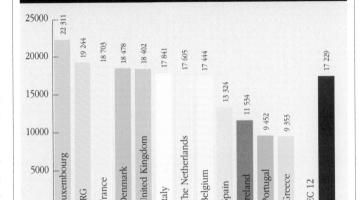

**GROSS DOMESTIC PRODUCT PER INHABITANT
(1989, IN STANDARD PURCHASING POWER)**

	Value
Luxembourg	22 311
FRG	19 244
France	18 703
Denmark	18 478
United Kingdom	18 402
Italy	17 841
The Netherlands	17 605
Belgium	17 444
Spain	13 324
Ireland	11 534
Portugal	9 452
Greece	9 353
EC 12	17 229

Source: Eurostat

THE BURDEN OF BELGIAN TAXATION

Taxation has come down since 1985.

FISCAL CHARGES AND LOCAL TAXES, AS % OF THE GNP					
	1960	1970	1980	1990	1991
Taxation	18.9	23.9	36.2	28.9	28.7
Direct tax	7.3	10.7	24.3	16.4	16.1
Indirect tax	11.4	12.7	11.6	12.2	12.2
Tax on capital	0.2	0.3	0.3	0.3	0.3
Social security contributions	7.1	10.3	13.6	14.7	15.2
Total	26.0	34.2	49.8	43.6	43.8

Source: Ministry of Finance

TAXATION IN THE EUROPEAN COMMUNITY (IN RELATION TO THE GNP)				
	1960	1970	1980	1990
Belgium	**26.3**	**34.2**	**42.0**	**42.6**
The Netherlands	30.4	40.8	46.3	46.5
Denmark	25.3	40.2	46.2	51.4
Germany	33.6	36.6	42.6	40.6
Luxembourg	30.3	32.0	47.1	47.7
France	33.4	37.0	42.6	44.3
Great Britain	27.3	37.7	37.0	35.2
Ireland	22.2	32.7	35.4	36.7
Italy	27.0	28.6	31.1	38.6
EG (*)	28.4	35.5	42.2	42.6

Source: Ministry of Finance
(*) Without Greece

Between 1960 and 1985, the average taxation levied (including local taxes) rose from 26% to 47%. This increase is explained by the need to finance growing expenditure, discretionary tax increases and the automatic increase as a result of the growth in the GNP. Taxation has come down since 1985.

In Europe the small countries pay the highest average taxes. These countries have also seen the fastest rise in taxation since 1960. Belgium held a middle position until 1970 but since 1975 has been among the top five. The rate of increase in Belgium between 1970 and 1985 was also above the EC average.

REGIONAL DIFFERENCES

Up until 1960, Belgian industry was centred in Wallonia and in the provinces of Hainaut and Liège in particular.

ECONOMIC PROFILE OF THE BOROUGHS

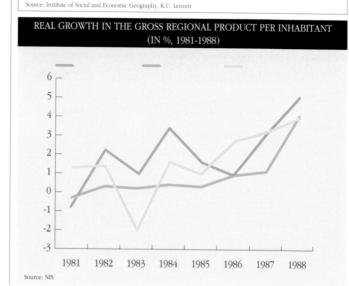

Boroughs with industry and service industries
Industrial boroughs
Prosperous, residential boroughs
Dormitory boroughs
Boroughs with service industries
Agricultural areas

Source: Institute of Social and Economic Geography, K.U. Leuven

REAL GROWTH IN THE GROSS REGIONAL PRODUCT PER INHABITANT (IN %, 1981-1988)

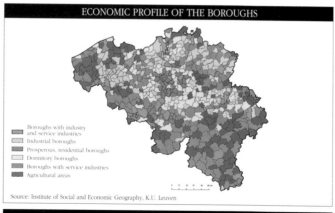

Source: NIS

Coal and steel manufacturing drew a whole chain of support companies to Wallonia. However, after 1960, it was mainly Flanders that experienced a true industrial revolution when it transferred from agriculture and light processing industries (such as textiles) to chemical industries, metal processing, electrotechnical companies and new technologies. Foreign investors were attracted by the sizeable labour reserve, the peaceful social climate, the relatively low wages and the good infrastructure. It was largely the sea ports and the Antwerp-Ghent-Brussels triangle that shared in the success, but big towns like Kortrijk, Hasselt, Liège and Charleroi were also growth areas. In Wallonia in general the new wave of investments was somewhat smaller, though the Walloon authorities are now trying all sorts of initiatives to restore growth to the region.

BEYOND THE BELGIAN BORDERS

The Belgian economy has always gravitated strongly towards foreign markets.

Around the turn of the century, for example, Belgian companies were involved in laying railways all over the world. The great demand from abroad was also largely responsible for the expansion of the "golden sixties". Foreign trade is of vital importance to the Belgian economy, but this also means that Belgium is very sensitive to the market developments of its major trade partners.

Belgium has no exportable natural raw materials. Consequently, its exports are mainly manufactured goods. Finished and half-finished products account for three-quarters of Belgian exports.

EMPHASIS ON EXPORT (EXPORT AS % OF TURNOVER) IN INDUSTRY IN 1990				
	Flanders	Wallonia	Brussels	Belgium
Raw materials	81.7	81.9	78.5	81.5
Building materials	30.5	46.1	51.4	40.3
Chemical industry	74.8	66.1	67.7	71.6
Metallurgy	66.0	62.3	61.0	64.3
Food-drinks-tobacco	37.1	30.6	49.2	37.6
Textile industry	83.3	74.3	72.2	82.2
Clothing	53.0	50.1	26.5	49.5
Timber	45.4	31.2	20.9	42.3
Paper-printing	47.0	56.2	27.4	45.4
Rubber and plastic	67.5	75.6	83.3	65.0
Miscellaneous	77.1	38.3	57.7	72.0

Source: N.I.S.

MOST IMPORTANT CLIENTS AND SUPPLIERS IN THE BLEU (1992, IN BILLIONS OF BEF)					
Clients			Suppliers		
	Output	% exported		Output	% imported
Germany	852	23.5	Germany	827	23.3
France	689	18.9	France	591	16.7
The Netherlands	540	13.7	The Netherlands	571	16.1
United Kingdom	486	13.3	United Kingdom	284	8.0
Italy	215	5.9	Italy	170	4.8

Source: N.I.S.

* **More than 80% of Belgian exports are destined for other European countries. Similarly, 80% of Belgian imports derive from other European countries.**

* **Between 1980 and 1989 imports rose by 85% and exports by 108%.**

* **In 1988 the Flemish Region was responsible for 74% of the industrial goods sent abroad, the Walloon Region for 22% and the Brussels Region for 5%.**

* **Belgium exports 12 billion francs worth of goods every working day.**

BORN EXPORTERS

*Belgian are born exporters :
on a worldwide scale,
they rank ninth among
the great commercial powers
and Belgium is even the leader
among the group
of industrialised nations
from the point of view
of exports per inhabitant.*

More than 10 000 of our companies export and, in most cases, they dispatch more than half of their output abroad.

Certain clear factors explain this remarkable success: the privileged location of the country and its well-developed roads infrastructure which allows fast and easy access to foreign companies, whether they be situated in Germany, France or in the Netherlands.

However, there is more: our centuries-old commercial tradition, our marked specialisation in certain types of products and the legendary flexibility of Belgian businessmen when dealing with their foreign partners are equally and without doubt so many reasons for the development of the phenomenon of Belgian exports.

Moreover, many Belgian companies have become leaders in a whole series of products at a European level and even at a world level; we may cite, among others, the example of buses, billiard balls, cyclotrons, diamonds, vaccines, pharmaceutical products,... sweets, Roentgen films, steel wire, transformers, carpeting, weaving looms or yachts.

However, exports are not limited simply to goods: the export of services also plays a very important role. Indeed, Belgian companies have built electric power stations in Mexico, factories for the production of telecommunications equipment in China, harbours in Thailand, hospitals in Russia, tower-blocks in the United Arab Emirates. Specialised Belgian companies are working on supplying the lighting system for the Channel tunnel, sailing-boats for Caribbean cruises or have been entrusted with the dredging of a the new harbour in Hong-Kong.

This success is, of course, worthy of the encouragement of a Prince. For more than twenty years, Prince Albert of Belgium, the brother of the King, in his capacity as President of the Belgian Office of Foreign Trade, has conducted missions with a view to encouraging exports to the five continents. Each year, the Prince awards an Oscar for Exports to a dozen Belgian entrepreneurial exporters. After all, the champions of exports also deserve "Oscars", whether they export carbonated water, telephone exchanges or banking software...

Prince Albert, presenting the 1991 Oscar for Exports to the Director of ATEA, the well-known exporter of telephones.

PROSPERITY

Belgium is a modern welfare state with a high average standard of living.

The vast majority of the population has any number of all sorts of luxury products. Over the last three decades, progress on that score has been spectacular.

Not only what and how much people eat, but also the changes in consumer habits tell us a great deal about living standards. Between 1970 and 1988 the proportion of incomes spent on food, drink and tobacco fell from 30% to 21%. It is known that the proportion of incomes spent on food decreases as living standards rise. A smaller proportion is spent on clothes, too. On the other hand, comparatively more is now spent on transport, communication and medical care.

* **97% of Belgian households have at least one television set.**

* **In 1988 energy consumption was 1482 kW. per inhabitant (Eur12: 1283).**

* **Each person uses on average 110 litres of water per day.**

* **The daily calorie intake of the average Belgian is in the region of 3 300.**

* **Each year 34 litres of Cola, 5 litres of fruit juice and 7 kg. of coffee are consumed per head of population in Belgium.**

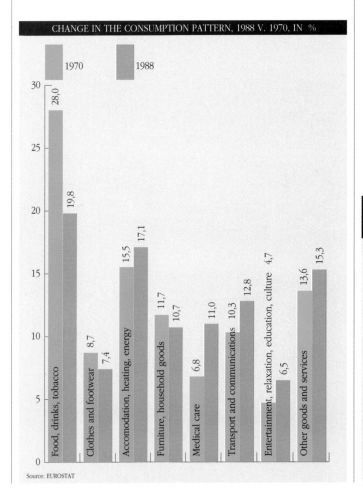

CHANGE IN THE CONSUMPTION PATTERN, 1988 V. 1970, IN %

1970   1988

Food, drinks, tobacco: 28,0 / 19,8
Clothes and footwear: 8,7 / 7,4
Accomodation, heating, energy: 15,5 / 17,1
Furniture, household goods: 11,7 / 10,7
Medical care: 6,8 / 11,0
Transport and communications: 10,3 / 12,8
Entertainment, relaxation, education, culture: 4,7 / 6,5
Other goods and services: 13,6 / 15,3

Source: EUROSTAT

CONSUMPTION OF AGRICULTURAL PRODUCTS (KG PER YEAR, PER INHABITANT, 1990)	
Wheat	69.3
Potatoes	91.1
Fruit	58.2
Vegetables	92.3
Sugar	42.3
Beef	16.9
Veal	3.0
Pork	45.8
Lamb/mutton	2.0
Chicken	14.2
Horse meat	3.0
Total for meat	90.6
Milk	69.3
Butter	7.7
Cheese	15.8
Eggs	13.8

Source: Agricultural Economic Institute

INCOMES

Most Belgians have an earned income. Office workers earn an average of 40% more than blue-collar workers.

BREAKDOWN OF SOCIAL SECURITY PAYMENTS (IN %)			
	1970	1980	1988
Pensions	34.5	35.2	34.5
Health care	31.4	30.3	32.1
Family allowances	22.4	13.6	10.5
Unemployment benefit	3.7	13.7	16.6
Other	8.0	7.2	6.3
Share in the GNP	13.0	19.6	19.5

Source: General Report of Social Security

In addition to an income from work, a high percentage of the population benefits from social services. These services have been planned with extreme care. Belgium is one of the countries (together with Luxembourg, the Netherlands, West Germany, France and Denmark) that spends more on social protection per head of the population than the European average. If the European average is 100 BEF, then Belgium spends 111 BEF. A large proportion of the expenditure on social security goes to senior citizens (35% in 1988), medical care (32%) and unemployment (17%).

* In 1991 the gross wage of a male blue-collar worker in industry averaged 374 BEF; for women it was 252 BEF. The gross monthly salary of a male white-collar worker in industry averaged in 1989 85 400 BEF; for women this was 54 900 BEF.

* The average pension is 49% of the last salary.

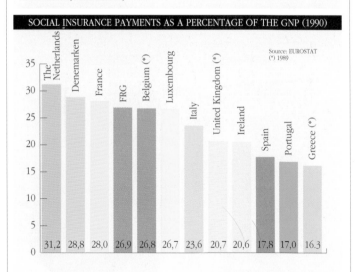

SOCIAL INSURANCE PAYMENTS AS A PERCENTAGE OF THE GNP (1990)

Source: EUROSTAT
(*) 1989

The Netherlands 31,2 — Denemarken 28,8 — France 28,0 — FRG 26,9 — Belgium (*) 26,8 — Luxembourg 26,7 — Italy 23,6 — United Kingdom (*) 20,7 — Ireland 20,6 — Spain 17,8 — Portugal 17,0 — Greece (*) 16.3

POVERTY

*One in five households is
financially insecure.*

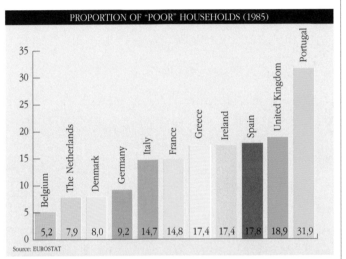

PROPORTION OF "POOR" HOUSEHOLDS (1985)

Belgium	The Netherlands	Denmark	Germany	Italy	France	Greece	Ireland	Spain	United Kingdom	Portugal
5,2	7,9	8,0	9,2	14,7	14,8	17,4	17,4	17,8	18,9	31,9

Source: EUROSTAT

Despite all the effort on the part of the Government to provide adequate and fair social protection, a high percentage of the population still finds itself living in financial insecurity.

Between one and four and one in five households is financially insecure and 5% (Eur12: 14%) is caught in the poverty trap. What is remarkable is that despite the 1976-1985 economic crisis, financial insecurity has not increased. However, we now find other groups hit. While senior citizens are more financially secure as a result of improved pension

PROPORTION OF THE BELGIAN POPULATION THAT CONSIDERS CERTAIN ITEMS NECESSARY, AND ITS POSSESSION OF THOSE ITEMS

Item	% which considers item as necessary	% not in possession of item
Coat	97.6	3.9
Damp-free housing	97.5	7.8
WC in the house	97.3	4.9
Heating in the living-room	96.9	3.1
Refrigerator	96.2	2.7
Meat or fish meal	94.0	4.9
Bath or shower	93.9	10.0
Washing-machine	91.6	11.4
Watertight shoes	89.8	9.3
Regular savings	84.5	39.4
Telephone	64.3	17.3
Car	58.1	24.3
One week's holiday	56.6	50.1
Colour TV	54.5	13.1
Central heating	45.2	36.3
Daily newspaper	31.1	54.0
Vacuum cleaner	79.5	10.4
Video recorder	8.1	75.5

Source: University of Antwerp, Center of Social Policy

schemes, the number of impecunious young people and unemployed has increased.

The Belgian social security system ensures that people do not fall below the poverty line. Unemployment benefits are ample and family allowances are generous and universal and these financial contributions reflect the cost of living. Finally, the guaranteed subsistence level acts as a safety net. All these factors contribute to there being proportionately fewer poor people in Belgium than in the other European countries.

THE BELGIANS

HOW MANY BELGIANS WORK?

The proportion of people employed is determined by the size of the population and the percentage of people in work.

The end of the seventies and the beginning of the eighties saw two trends: more young people were looking for jobs, while only a small number of old people were retiring. This coincided with the cut in jobs in industry and led to a sharp rise in unemployment. Today we have a different picture. Many people are dropping out of the work-force and relatively few young people are looking for work. Consequently, the population at working age has stabilised since the mideighties. It is now even beginning to fall.

In recent years the employment rate among men (the number of men that actually work) has fallen, at least among the younger and older age groups. The figure for 25-50 year-old men is fairly stable. The drop in the number of young people is linked to longer schooling and the drop in the number of old people to early pensions. The employment rate as a whole among men is on the decrease. However, this is not the case with women where the number of working 20-45 year-olds has increased over the last few decades, a trend that is set to continue for some time to come. The total employment rate among women is on the increase. It is called "feminization" of the workforce.

* **The number of people employed by the Government out of the total working population was 25% in 1991 (in 1970: 14%).**

* **The number of women in the total workforce was 40% in 1991 and 32% in 1970.**

* **After the Second World War, three out of ten 25-29 year-old women went out to work; now it is eight out of ten.**

* **After the Second World War, seven out of ten 60 to 64 year-old males went out to work; now it is just two out of ten.**

In 1974, 3 750 000 people worked. In 1984, that number fell to 3 540 000 which means that 200 000 jobs were lost in the space of ten years. The situation began to change in 1985. In the period 1985-88, the number of jobs increased by 100 000, though there were big differences between men and women. Between 1974 and 1988, the number of working males fell by almost 300 000 but the number of working women increased by 160 000. The number of self-employed and the number of "helpers" (family members who contribute but are unpaid) remained unchanged between 1975 and 1985. This group has been growing since then and the number of self-employed people is now about 20%. It is in the service sector that the number of self-employed people is increasing, while in industry it remains stable and in agriculture it is falling.

Between 1974 and 1988, almost 500 000 jobs were lost in industry (where four out of five jobs were taken by men). In the service sector, which employs a high percentage of women, 360 000 jobs were created. This is mainly the result of an increase in jobs in the government sector, where 120 000 additional jobs were created between 1974 and 1988. Almost 1 000 000 Belgians now work in the public sector.

WHERE DO PEOPLE WORK ?

During the 1960 to 1974 economic heyday, more than 200 000 jobs were created.

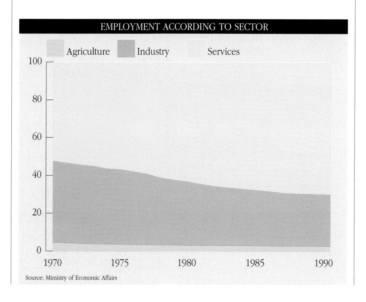

EMPLOYMENT ACCORDING TO SECTOR

Agriculture   Industry   Services

Source: Ministry of Economic Affairs

* **Working-hours have been greatly reduced: only 38 to 39 hours remain of the former 45-hour working week. The length of the annual holiday has increased from 3 weeks in the sixties to more than one month today. Part-time work has also increased. The proportion of part-time work in the national employment total rose from 3% in 1973 to 11% in 1989. Part-time work is particularly popular among women: 23% of female workers are employed on a part-time basis.**

* **Three out of four self-employed pursue these activities as their main activity.**

* **90% of part-time jobs are in the service sector**

* **Nine out of ten female workers are employed in the service sector.**

* **27% of the self-employed are women.**

* **The government sector employs 52% men and 48% women.**

* **The Flemish Region provides 59% of the jobs in private employment, the Walloon Region 24% and the Brussels Region 17%.**

* **In 1989 there were 52 183 male and 3 188 female professional servicemen and 34 687 males doing their military service.**

THE BELGIANS

MOBILITY

Belgium has more than 50 km of motorway per 1 000 km². No other Western European country can match Belgium in this respect.

The motorways remain lit throughout the night and this is unique. It also means that Belgium can be accurately located from outer space. Only the Great Wall of China has the same reputation! Astronauts talk about "The Belgian Window". The motorways near the large cities are usually built as ring roads which considerably helps the traffic flow. Nevertheless, the large cities with their historic centres still have to contend with severe problems of congestion.

There have been cut-backs in the railway network over the last two decades. Less profitable lines have been dispensed with in favour of more important international intercity and inter-regional routes. The secondary lines, which are heavily used by commuters, have been improved. Most train lines converge on Brussels. Every day hundreds of thousands of Belgians commute to and from the capital city. However, a number of central services have been transferred to smaller towns in an effort to solve the traffic problems.

The Changing World Of Agriculture

The number of farmers has fallen sharply in recent decades. Agriculture now accounts for only 3% of the labour force.

Agriculture employs some 90 000 people on a permanent basis. A further 55 000 are employed on a non-permanent basis. There is also less land given over to agriculture: between 1960 and 1985, almost 270 000 ha. of agricultural land were lost, or 16% of the total. This loss is largely the result of urbanisation projects, industrialisation and road-building, especially in Flanders. Less agricultural land has been lost in recent years.

Some 45% of Belgium's total surface area is given over to agriculture (Eur12: 57%). The average unit is 15 ha. (20 ha. per (professional) farm, 3 ha. in the horticulture sector). In the Flemish Region the average area is 10 ha., in the Brussels Region 12 ha. and in the Walloon Region 25 ha. The Eur12 average is 12 ha. By comparison: in the USA it is 180 ha. and in Australia 2 700 ha.

Despite the drop in the number of farmers and the loss of agricultural land, agricultural production has increased. This is the result of specialisation, better vocational training, intensive agricultural research, improved production methods and the rationalisation of distribution.

Livestock accounts for 66% of total agricultural production, horticulture (especially market gardening) for 18% and arable production (corn) 15%. Livestock is bred intensively in areas where there is plentiful pasture land such as the polders, the Famenne, the Antwerp Kempen, the Herve region and the Oosten van Condroz. There are more than 3.1 million head of cattle, of which under a third are dairy cows, and 6.7 million pigs (95% of which are in the Flemish Region).

Belgium also has a good reputation for its vegetables, some 80% of which are produced for export. Most famous of all is Belgian chicory which is exported to 40 countries, but (house) plants and flowers also do well. Belgium is the largest azalea producer in the world and 60% of Europe's total production of begonias comes from Belgium.

---

* **One Belgian farmer provides food for 80 consumers.**

---

* **Belgium has over 14 are of agricultural land per inhabitant.**

---

* **Agriculture represents 2.5% of the GNP and 6% of exports.**

---

* **58% of Belgian agricultural land is used for breeding livestock.**

---

* **One third of Belgian pork is exported.**

---

* **60% of farm managers are more than 50 years old.**

---

* **The Flemish Region has 60 m² of public woodland per inhabitant, the Walloon Region 766 m² and the Brussels Region 0.17 m².**

SEA FISHING

*Belgian fishing is concentrated
in the ports of Zeebrugge,
Ostend and Nieuwpoort.
There are now fewer ships
than before; however, the gross
tonnage remains unchanged
and the volume of the catches
per ship has increased.
The industry also tries to satisfy
the growing demand for quality
fish which is to be found mainly
outside the coastal waters.
Belgian sea-fishing is subject
to quotas which are fixed for
each E.C. Member State so as
to ensure that stocks of certain
sorts of fish (e.g. herrings and
sole) are maintained.*

*Fishing on
horseback in
Oostduinkerke*

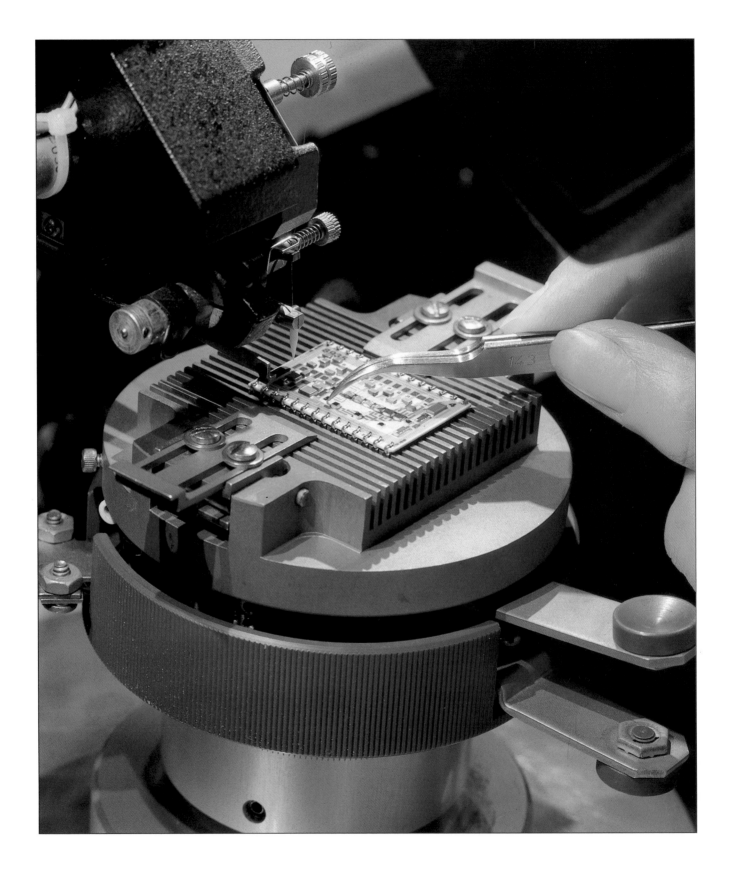

MODERNISED INDUSTRIES

*In the nineteenth century,
Belgium was the first country
on the European Continent
to be caught up in the
industrial revolution
which had started
in Great Britain.*

Not that Belgium had to start from scratch. Ever since the Middle Ages, Flanders had had a well-developed cotton industry and Wallonia had experience in arms manufacture and metal construction work. In Wallonia there were also coal reserves which had been mined since the thirteenth century, albeit on a small scale.

Between 1840 and 1880, the annual growth in industrial production often reached more than 5%. The number of people employed in industry rose from 406 000 in 1846 to 1 069 000 in 1910. Nevertheless, the First World War, and to a lesser extent the Second, had a disastrous influence on the industrial apparatus. After 1945, Belgium was successful in attracting substantial investments. Industrial expansion took place mainly in the chemical sector, metal industry, wood and furniture industry, energy sector and the glass industry. Growth was concentrated mainly in Flanders where

great efforts were made to adapt existing industrial structures and to diversify. The old industrial areas of Wallonia, on the other hand, went into decline. Since 1957, 118 coal mines have been closed, including all the mines in Wallonia (the last mine was closed on September 30th 1984). Two coal mines in the Kempen are still operative but are due to close in 1993. A number of textile and clothing companies have also

disappeared because they could not compete with the low-wage countries and the introduction of new man-made fibres. The steel industry has also been hard hit.

Between 1960 and 1974, annual industrial growth averaged 5.4%, or a doubling of industrial output within 14 years. The chemical sector, wood, metal processing, machine building and the steel industry scored even

better with growth figures of around 8 to 10%. Non-ferrous metals, food, textiles and the agricultural sector were below the average. During the course of the next decade, industrial production stagnated and the average annual growth was barely 0.6%. Only the chemical industry managed to sustain high growth figures. The non-ferrous industry, metal production, food and paper were able to sustain positive growth. All other sectors saw a negative growth and Belgian companies became less and less competitive. Many had to close down, lay off or reorganise staff. Between 1974 and 1982, 381 000 jobs were lost in industry, which was 25% of the total. In 1982, the Government intervened by devaluing the franc, imposing a pay freeze and establishing favourable conditions for attracting risk capital. This produced results. Companies became more competitive and from 1985 onwards investments in production increased.

ENTERPRISING BELGIUM

INDEX FIGURES FOR INDUSTRIAL OUTPUT PER SECTOR (INDEX 1985=100)				
	1970	1980	1990	1991
General				
General (excl. construction)	97.0	110.1	122.4	116.9
General (incl. construction)	77.1	95.9	117.7	115.0
Per sector				
Extraction industry	215.7	118.8	38.1	27.0
Food + drinks industry	64.9	86.2	117.5	118.2
Tobacco	79.2	96.0	86.1	91.2
Textile industry	106.2	96.2	112.4	104.4
Clothing	116.5	108.6	118.3	123.6
Timber industry	58.9	104.6	135.3	144.4
Paper + cardboard	72.5	88.8	130.0	125.3
Chemical + rubber industry	55.6	85.5	128.5	130.5
Iron + steel industry	110.6	112.4	108.4	107.5
Non-ferrous industry	69.0	100.2	121.8	112.6
Metal processing industry	73.3	95.0	120.7	116.1
Electrical industry	53.4	94.3	124.1	125.3
Water distribution	67.1	91.3	101.1	105.0
Construction industry	254.5	186.8	142.9	124.7

Source: N.I.S.

* The importance of industry in the national economy has fallen from 45% in 1960 to 28% today

* 98% of private companies are small and medium-sized enterprises (i.e. 100 employees or fewer). Just over 70% of them employ fewer than five people. The total contribution of these enterprises to the employment market is 47%.

* Between 1980 and 1988, industrial production in the Flemish Region increased by 22%, by 2% in the Brussels Region and in the Walloon Region production remained stable.

TURNOVER AND NET PROFIT OF THE 50 LARGEST COMPANIES (ACCORDING TO TURNOVER, 1990, IN MILLIONS OF BEF)			
	Turnover	Net profit	Net profit/turnover
1 Petrofina	577 692	22 466	0.039
2 Delhaize De Leeuw	266 172	7 040	0.026
3 Solvay	255 241	15 910	0.062
4 GIB Group	205 418	2 993	0.015
5 Cockerill Sambre	203 110	12 467	0.061
6 Electrabel	183 076	22 249	0.122
7 Ford Belgium	149 262	nb	/
8 Esso/Exxon Belgium	129 702	2 409	0.019
9 Acec-Union Minière	120 550	3 820	0.032
10 Wagon-Lits	98 497	762	0.008
11 Volvo Belgium	93 238	3 451	0.037
12 RTT	90 026	9 721	0.108
13 Bayer-Belgium	86 345	4 976	0.058
14 Philips Belgium	73 276	nb	/
15 Renault Belgium	72 200	956	0.013
16 Volkswagen Belgium	71 028	2 184	0.031
17 BP Belgium	64 416	1 172	0.018
18 BASF Belgium	63 303	940	0.015
19 General Motors	60 118	3 210	0.053
20 Interbrew	58 376	2 293	0.039
21 Bekaert	56 991	-454	-0.008
22 NMBS	54 909	961	0.018
23 Sidmar	54 747	2 524	0.046
24 Gechem	52 646	1 090	0.021
25 Delhaize Louis	53 320	322	0.006
26 CMB	51 330	1 133	0.022
27 Distrigas	50 806	863	0.017
28 Shell Belgium	50 764	75	0.001
29 Post Office	50 116	472	0.009
30 UCB	43 360	2 308	0.053
31 Sabena	43 246	nb	/
32 CBR	43 233	4 501	0.104
33 d'Ieteren	42 750	1 825	0.043
34 Siemens Belgium	40 789	1 756	0.043
35 Tessenderlo Chemie	40 649	2 148	0.053
36 Nafta Belgium	40 570	156	0.004
37 Fiat Belgium	40 338	-256	-0.006
38 Vandemoortele	40 033	nb	/
39 Makro	38 219	123	0.003
40 Monsanto Europe	37 545	1 293	0.034
41 IBM Belgium	37 444	2 067	0.055
42 Tiense Suiker	37 127	1 908	0.051
43 Marubeni	35 390	73	0.002
44 PSA Belgium	35 349	165	0.005
45 Caterpillar	34 801	-1 080	-0.031
46 Aldi	34 566	984	0.028
47 Colruyt	32 334	859	0.027
48 Mitsui	28 682	63	0.002
49 Pioneer Belgium	28 833	796	0.028
50 Glaverbel	27 232	2 343	0.086

Bron: Trends

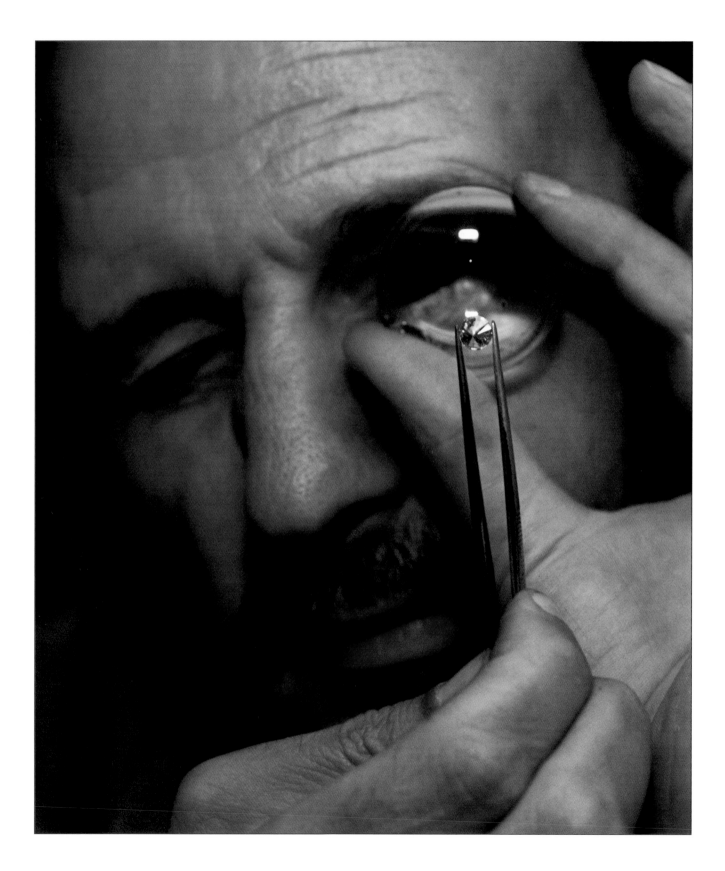

A DIAMOND IS FOR EVER

Centred mainly in and around Antwerp, the diamond industry is Belgium's pride and joy.

Antwerp has the largest diamond market in the world and is the most important world centre for the processing of large, high-quality stones. What is more, it was a Belgian, Lodewijk van Berckem from Bruges (15th century), who invented diamond polishing. There are six diamond schools in Antwerp. Trading revolves around four diamond exchanges. More than 95% of the diamonds are exported, mainly to the USA, Japan and Hong Kong. In these countries "Cut in Antwerp" is synonymous with quality.

The world's smallest, traditionally-polished diamond is Belgian. It weighs 0.0006 karats and its 0.58 mm. diameter has 57 facets.

TRANSPORT

COMMUNICATIONS NETWORKS (IN KM)			
	1970	1980	1990
Railways	4 165	3 971	3 479
Waterways	1 572	1 574	1 506
Road links	12 109	14 331	14 421
incl. motorways	411	1 203	1 631
Local railways	13 578	26 811	30 736
Tramlines, trolley bus lines etc.	1 577	1 840	1 615
Pipelines	50	460	286

Source: Ministry of Transport, Ministry of Public Works

GOODS TRANSPORT, ACCORDING TO MEANS OF TRANSPORT (IN BILLION TONNES PER KM)			
	1970	1980	1990
Road	12.8	15.7	25.2*
Rail	7.8	8.5	8.4
Inland waterways	6.7	6.0	5.5

Source: NIS

NUMBER OF SHIPS DOCKING PER PORT						
	1970	1980	1982	1984	1986	1990
Antwerp						
Number	19 150	17 151	17 097	16 802	16 446	14 989
Tonnage (*)	54 315	102 696	112 683	116 829	126 982	133 344
Ghent						
Number	3 214	3 260	3 407	4 786	4 469	3 713
Tonnage (*)	4 475	15 701	18 674	21 675	21 010	23 793
Bruges-Zeebrugge						
Number	4 691	9 550	8 625	9 775	10 085	10 868
Tonnage (*)	9 670	48 212	39 287	41 106	42 451	67 077

Source: Municipality of Antwerp, Port Authority, Municipality of Ghent Port Authority,
Bruges Shipping Authority
(*) for 1970 in BNT (Belgian Nett Tonnes); from 1980 in 1000 GRT (Gross Register Tonnes)

Years ago, most industries were located in the towns or on the main waterways and railway links to ensure easy transport of raw materials. Today, more and more industrial zones are being set up beside large transport infrastructures (ports and above all motorways) and on the outskirts of large towns. In Belgium there are about 500 industrial zones, together covering about 40 000 ha. Most new industries are set up in these zones. In the period 1955-1986, 40% of total state investment in transport infrastructure went onroads, 34% on public transport and 27% on waterways. Sixty-one percent of goods transport is by road, 21% by rail, 51% over the waterways and 3% by pipeline.

ENERGY

Its economic structure and climate make Belgium a high energy consumer. Over the years, the country has built up an enormous amount of expertise in the fields of exploration, production, transport and distribution of energy.

Petrofina, an oil and petrochemical holding company with branches in 25 countries throughout the world, plays a major role in this sector.

Until 1960, (Belgian) coal provided the main source of energy in Belgium. Then oil became more important. In 1973, oil provided 85% of Belgium's total energy, compared with coal's 13%. Gas and oil exploration was carried out in the whole of Belgium, but to no avail. It became clear from the oil crises of 1973-74 and 1979-81 that diversification was called for and coal, this time imported, was given a second chance. More gas was used as well, with the Netherlands, Norway and Algeria as its most important suppliers. Since the end of the seventies, gas has supplied about a fifth of the country's total energy needs. Electricity also plays a large role in the modern welfare state, representing around a fifth of the total energy used. Belgium has only limited potential in terms of water power which means that most of the electricity plants are fed by other sources of energy. Until the beginning of the sixties, that was mainly Belgian coal, later it was natural gas and petroleum. But since the 1973 oil crisis, there has been a move towards the faster development of nuclear plants for producing electricity. The first nuclear plant in Doel (along the River Scheldt, near Antwerp) came into operation in 1974. In 1975 a second plant was opened in Tihange (on the River Meuse, 30 km. upriver from Liège). Both units were expanded later on. There are now seven nuclear plants which together account for 70% of the electricity produced.

SERVICES: AN AREA OF ECONOMIC GROWTH

The service sector consists of a range of economic activities which share the common characteristic of producing intangible, incorporeal goods.

In 1970, 52% of the population was employed in the service sector; now it is 70%. The main area of growth in the service sector is in the so-called public sector (also called the soft, non-profit or non-market sector). It is the sector that makes goods and services available outside the market-place, without the need for the customer to pay (a price) for them in actual monetary terms. This sector accounts for almost 30% of all jobs. Its growth can also be explained by the fact that in the seventies the Government recognised

its potential for reducing unemployment.

The service sector comprises many heterogeneous activities and is growing in almost all areas. This so-called "tertiarization" is also making inroads into agriculture and industry. All large industrial enterprises have major commercial and advertising activities. In most

cases they also have financial, legal and information technology departments. A number undertake their own research or take part in research projects, sometimes together with universities.

Telecommunications also play an important role here. The importance of telecommunications to the econo-

my makes itself felt in all areas: transport, storage, distribution, financial aspects, research, etc. The tremendous internationalization of services is a fairly recent phenomenon.

* **In 1991 the number employed in public utilities (both national and regional) was 192 000; this represents 22% of all public employment.**

* **Three-quarters of the jobs in the tertiary sector are concentrated in the towns.**

THE FINANCIAL SECTOR

At world level, Belgium is an important financial centre. This is apparent from its many banks, the size of transactions on the stock exchange and the related ancillary businesses, such as insurance, leasing companies and investment funds. Many of these international activities are centred in Brussels.

To the south of Brussels, in Terhulpen, is the headquarters of SWIFT, the Society for Worldwide Interbank Financial Telecommunication. It is a company specialised in electronic message-processing and transmission services between financial institutions throughout the world. SWIFT was founded in 1973 and had four members of staff. Its first transaction dates back to 1977. Today SWIFT has 650 employees. It is the heart of a world telecommunications network that coordinates the transmission of hundreds of thousands of payment transfers to more than 60 countries and 1 300 banks.

In the financial sector, too, we are beginning to see internationalisation on a large scale: 67 of the 90 private banks with offices in Belgium are foreign-owned or largely so. Big, foreign financial holding companies have considerable interests in the Belgian economy.

DEVELOPMENT OF PAYMENT TRANSFERS

	1970	1980	1990	1991
Cheques used (millions)	36.4	111.8	100.3	96.7
Bank cards (thousands)	375	1 686	2 080	2 070
Payment cards issued (thousands)	/	834	5 157	5 358
(Bancontact, Mister Cash)				
Cash dispensers (Bancontact, Mister Cash)				
Number of dispensers	/	392	831	959
Number of withdrawals (thousands)	/	6 701	72 168	79 300
N°. of withdrawals per day per dispenser	/	46.8	237.9	226.5
Payment terminals				
Number of terminals	/	73	21 238	21 806
N°. of transactions (thousands)	/	134	71 562	94 800
N°. of transactions per day per terminal	/	5.0	9.2	11.9

Source: Association of Belgian Banks

TOTAL AMOUNT OF MONEY (AT END OF YEAR IN BILLIONS OF BEF) AND ANNUAL INCREASE

	1970	1980	1985	1987	1989	1990	1991
Currency in circulation	191	371	384	413	423	420	407
Transferable money	228	494	616	730	873	948	902
Owned by companies and							
private persons	203	445	561	677	794	874	794
Owned by the state	25	49	55	53	79	74	108
Total	419	865	1000	1143	1296	1368	1309
Annual increase as a %	8.4	0.3	6.3	4.1	8.2	5.5	-4.3

Source: NBB

CHAPTER

6

DIVERSITY & CULTURAL INNOVATION

CULTURE

*The cultural scene in Belgium
enjoys an international
reputation for its mixture of skill,
flights of fancy, tradition
and dynamism.*

This blend of unbridled creative power and age-old craftmanship has produced benefits in terms of knowledge and made a contribution to the art of good living as well. It goes without saying that it would take more than the few pages available here to take in the entire range of the cultural scene in Belgium, so a detailed analysis has to make way for a few sketches of the main features, and offer the reader a mere impression rather than a lengthy discourse. In this context, it is hardly feasible to seek to divide the communities into two opposing cultures. Belgium is first and foremost a land of movement and cultural exchange. Admittedly, the culture is not national, but nor is it exclusively regional, for the movements that have inspired the arts in Belgium have been international in their outlook, coming from nowhere because they come from everywhere. In a country whose borders have been as fluid as its history is fickle, trying to pin a culture down to one area would seem to have little sense. Art here may have escaped the conditions governing "belgitude", but it is still immersed in that state of mind which adores derision, humour and craftmanship.

Art in our regions is the external sign of an internal life teeming with rich ideas. A combination of technical skill and intense thought, art as a mirror of the soul also has to reflect the concerns of its age. The Belgian temperament can be recognised in the primitive painters who, like Van Eyck, brought to their work an attention to detail interpreted after mature reflection. The importance of these representations does not exclusively lie in the illusion, but also in the symbolic value it conveys. This gave rise to a tradition that was to be renewed by symbolism (Khnopff, Degouve de Nuncques, Spilliaert) and surrealism (Magritte, Delvaux). This tradition left its mark on art life in Belgium. Art lies in the gradual shift that the imagination imposes between the form and the thing being represented, between the word and the meaning. The pipe is no longer simply a pipe. Be it literary, musical or visual, the image opens a window onto the absolute. This culture is characterized by a quest for meanings, which sometimes becomes sarcasm through a negation of the self. A strange mixture of a desire for the absolute, and a need to deny what has

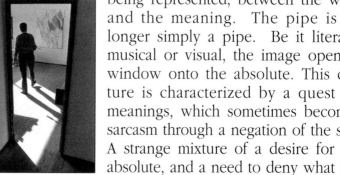

Van Lint

Dan Van Severen

been achieved, one part of the creative spirit in Belgium has continually used sham humility to cast a critical eye on the present. From the post-Zozos in Liège to the successors of Duchamp in Flanders, the extraordinary here is set up as a universal principle and paradox takes on a sweet flavour.

Ensuring the success of symbolism and surrealism in Belgium, this quest for the absolute is accompanied by a need for an identity, a need which is all the more intense because of historical circumstances which have often been tragic in our regions. The identity is a cultural one in the north of the country, whereas in the south it is focused more on social ties. Seen from the outside, the impression is gained that because of its hybrid character the confines of the Belgian territory were exempted early on from the need to have a set of characteristics according to which each artist could be classified. An extraordinary power of imagination and a marked aversion for tradition have been the hallmarks of the work produced by the famous names in the Belgian art world. For many Magritte and Broodthaers, among others, were

inspired by a spirit of derision which made their critical work all the more incisive. In Belgian art a caustic wit can be glimpsed peeking out, rejecting avant-garde clichés and the dictates of dogma. Conceptualism, minimalism, land art, neo-expressionism or a return to abstraction are not to be seen as artistic expressions as such, but as subjective expressions of their critical power (Guillaume Bijl, Thierry de Cordier, André Stas, etc.) In our regions, be they in the north or in the south of the country, there is to be found the same persistent questioning: an interaction between language and image disturbed by the mind (Jan Vercruysse, Jacques Charlier, Patrick Corillon, etc.); the mythical situation of a work at the centre of the imaginary (Jephan de Villiers, Wim Delvoye, Panamarenko, etc.), the searching doubts of the artist laying his soul bare in his work (Pasternak, Marchoul, etc.), the exploration of a powerful gesture conveying inner depths from which myths and memories of the past rise to the surface (Jan Cox, Pierre Alechinsky, Serge Vandercam, Gabriel Belgeonne, Xiao-Xia, etc.).

Jo Delahaut

In the French-speaking part of the country, the stringent demands of symbolism allied with the cavalier attitude of surrealism have the effect of making dogmatism taboo, whilst ensuring that subjective mystery continues to play a part in what is created. The humour bespeaks by turns a sense of modesty, a feeling of anger, an invitation to complicity or a desire to shock. The world of the comic strip (from Franquin to Peyo) or the plastic arts from Pol Bury to Jacques Lizène have both produced a few masters in their fields. Derision does duty as a manifesto. It seeks to challenge the primacy of language and the permanence of history and the direction it has taken has close literary parallels.

On the other side of the language border, the image finds its plastic values once again: abstraction has had its moments of glory in Belgium. From its very beginnings, Flanders has found there the terms of a universal language (Seuphor, de Boeck, Vantongerloo). After 1945, the end of the war announ-ced a profound change (Jo Delahaut, Marc Mendelson, Louis Van Lint, Anne Bonnet..). The Young Belgian Painter Movement won renown in this context. In its wake, Cobra exposed the senses to abstraction by exploring the paths of the unconscious and the word. Illustrated through gestures and a different way of regarding the image, abstraction inspired works drenched in colour, with the raw flesh of the imagination being portrayed in one or two energetic flourishes (Bram Bogaert, Antoine Mortier, Jan Cox). Other artists, more interested in the adventures of the mind, imposed order and moderation, with the senses being maintained in a state of balance. Abstraction also took the form of dispassionate geometrical design (Jo Delahaut, Marthe Wéry, Michel Mouffe...). The plane breathes and the space expands around these finished designs which result in new forms of abstraction, viz. the installation (Ludwig Vandevelde) or the total oeuvre (Jan Fabre).

Strip cartoon artist Morris

The artistic scene is also influenced by the policies of the cultural bodies intended to support it. It rests at the same time on a political project and on an aesthetic intention. When exposing his Chambres d'amis (Guest Rooms) in 1986, Jan Hoet, the head of the Modern Art Museum in Ghent, queried the whole purpose of the traditional museum, echoing the same sort of sentiments expressed before him by Broodthaers when setting up his Musée d'Art moderne - Département des aigles (Modern Art Museum - Department of Eagles). The affirmation of the artist implied a transformation of the cultural venues. The idea behind this ambitious plan was to get art closer to the people by establishing a new and decentralised policy. One or two of the initiatives have already enjoyed some success: the boost to the reputation of the Modern Art Museum in Ghent has earned its director the enviable title of Kunstlerischer Leiter of the Dokumenta IX in Kassel; specialising in contemporary sculpture, the Atelier 340 in Brussels has made a name for itself not only as a place for research but also as a respected centre of cultural activity. The centres for artistic expression found throughout Wallonia are helping to re-establish a link between the general public and creativity: the focus on photography in Charleroi, engraving in La Louvière, cartoon strips in Brussels, tapestry in Tournai, pottery in Villers-la-Ville, goldsmith's trade in Seneffe, provides each of these disciplines with an anchorage point and an opportunity to develop. This boost to the arts has been heightened by an increase in the number of cultural bodies: examples are a Modern Art Museum attached to the Belgian Royal Museums of Fine Art in Brussels, a Modern Art Museum in Antwerp, a Provincial Museum of Modern Art in Ostend and Hasselt, a space devoted to modern art in Liège).

This widespread policy of decentralisation has helped to promote the present revival of contemporary art in Belgium. The commercial channels are extending and there has been a rise in the number of galleries opening, some of which now enjoy an international reputation (Fred Lanzenberg, Isy Brachot, Albert Baronian, Plus Kern in Brussels, Micheline Szwajcer in Antwerp; Elisabeth Franck and André Simoens in Knokke-het-Zoute; and many others spread around the country). Art critics from abroad are now showing an interest in what is happening in this two-community nation: the Biennial in Venice, the Belgian Art Scene exhibition staged in 1990 at the Modern Art Museum in Paris, the International Exhibition of Contemporary Art organised in the same city the following year - all of these events displayed a similar interest in what is going on in Belgium. Moreover, the individual language-communities see to it that their own cultural images are made known throughout the world, which only goes to further strengthen their specific images inside the country.

Though art continues to be international in outlook, it is worth underscoring the importance invested in identity as a basis for this creative activity nurtured on the recognition it receives abroad. Belgium grew out of the culture of the 19th century and now sees its destiny taking shape at the crossroads of modern nations. But it is to the arts that it turns in order to discover its inner meaning. Caught between a need to be forward-looking and a desire to explore its roots, Belgian creativity is faced with a set of paradoxes.

Panamarenko

Curator
Jan Hoet

Ever since the end of the 19th century, Flanders has felt a need to revive its old traditions. In this quest for its roots, Flanders has forged itself an identity through a renewed interest in its literature. The Lion of Flanders, one of the masterpieces of Flemish literature, was taken up by Henri Conscience as a theme for rekindling the memory of a once-mighty Flanders, imposing its language as a ferment for an original culture which discovered in Guido Gezelle its poet. Whilst the flight into the absolute induced those like Maeterlinck and Verhaeren to turn towards French culture, the Flemish identity called for a celebration of its origins. These were rooted in the land, the image of which painters of Sint-Martens-Latem (Constant Permeke, Gustaaf De Smet and Frits Van den Berghe) spread on canvas in expressionist impasto. This quest for an identity mixed past and present by combining the memory of a people with the artist's questioning mind. The post-war years were influenced by existentialism and Flemish literature embarked upon an exploration of the unconsciousness, calling into question an ossified tradition and favouring freedom of the senses and sensation (Hugo Claus, Paul Snoek). This movement placed itself on the fringe of a traditional society so as to cast a critical eye and leave people with uneasy consciences (Louis-Paul Boon). It was the inspiration for an experimental form of theatre whose hallmark was the absurd and cruelty (Tone Brulin). Come the 1960s, writers were wielding their pens like lethal weapons (Fernand Auwera) and Flemish literature embarked upon the path of neo-realism and modernism producing works bursting with imagery. There developed a pressing need to achieve a synthesis of the arts. The theatre sought to intensify expressionist experiences and transform action into a form of choreography in which masquerade, pantomime, song and the plastic arts were all

Author Pierre Mertens

brought into service. In the 1970s, a crisis of conscience began to emerge and this was made all the more intense because the rallying cries were becoming lost in the absurdity of political speculation. As a result, Flemish literature handed over the responsibility for political challenges to souls lost in confusion (Hugo Raes). Language became in itself a privileged sanctuary, whilst the artist remained aloof from the monotonous political merry-go-round to express in writing his misgivings about mankind. During the 1980s this poetic investigation of language began to assert itself, throwing a powerful mythical light on the autobiographical questioning of the Flemish intellectuals. The language became flamboyant and renewed its contact with ancestral traditions which had come to be seen as the only stable reference points.

In the south of the country, the major social conflicts, the challenges of democracy and a powerful literary tradition have made it possible to play in a varied range of keys: whether it be a question of political commitment and its libertarian negation, inextricably linked to surrealism (Paul Nougé, Achille Chavée, Marcel Lecomte, E.L.T. Mesens or Louis Scutenaire), the social, indeed even sociological, explorations of Georges Simenon or the need to give a personal view of the fleeting impressions of life, Belgian writing can boast some of the finest treasures in the French language. The high quality of the work produced is seemingly due to the pleasure taken in practising the craft and the sense of balance worthy of a miniaturist in the choice of words. It is no coincidence that two of the most important grammarians of the French language are of Belgian nationality; the "Dictionnaire des difficultés du français moderne" by Joseph Hanse and "Le Bon Usage" by Maurice Grévisse have not only become classics in their field, but are also a sign of a commitment to the purity

CHAPTER 6

CULTURAL DIVERSITY & INNOVATION

of language with all the precision this implies.

Intent on finding the exact expression, literature in the French-speaking community is not indifferent either to a subjective exploitation of this quest for perfection in the language. The neo-classical rigour of the methods means that there is a temptation to veer towards the baroque. During the 1960s post-war illusions were being dispelled, whilst the literary scene underwent a transformation. In search of fresh values, individuals set about interpreting the signs of institutional change in the new Belgium. Just like in Flanders, writers in the French-language community embarked upon an exploration of this world without landmarks in a bid to discover the expression of their new identity, torn as they were between "belgitude" (a term coined by the writer Pierre Mertens) and a fascination with the Parisian glamour. The sense of unease in Belgium is felt not only by the intelligentsia. The most resounding expression of this malaise was to be found in the work of someone whose message was heard across the whole country, someone whose extraordinary talent will long be remembered, and that person is Jacques Brel.

The slow decay of the national state has had a destabilising effect on people's attitudes and overturned the old certainties. The process lends itself to fictional interpretation: sparking off a fantastic picture with fiction becoming stranger than reality (Jean Ray, Frans Hellens), or a critical view when an author associates the process with the destiny of society and its myths (Suzanne Lilar, Charles Bertin). An uncompromising derisory stance, "Le Dérisoire Absolu "(Pierre Alechinsky and Pol Bury) puts people at risk when reason seems to desert a state intent on its own destruction. This has had the effect of making writers in the French-speaking community seem to vacillate between a disillusioned exploration of history and an internalisation of the subjective values of language. As poetry makes itself felt as the pre-eminent literary form for an intimate dialogue (Fernand Verhesen, Philippe Jones, Claire Lejeune...), the novel (Gaston Compère, Pierre Mertens...) is asserting itself in parallel with the theatre (Paul Willems, Henry Bauchau...), which, in the French-speaking part of the country, is riding on the crest of a wave. Language becomes a mirror of the times, a key for a derision designed to mask disenchantment (Jacques Sojcher, Raoul Vaneigem) or utter indifference (Jean-Claude Pirotte, Philippe Toussaint). Writing has become a symbol of elegance located on the fringes of a "Pays Noyé", whose ephemeral destiny is sketched out in the work of Paul Willems.

This culture is theatrical because of its ability to offer itself up to scrutiny and because of a vitality allowing it to step back and take a critical look at itself. It is no accident then that the theatre is in an exceptionally healthy state. In Flanders, it was the "Vlaamse Volkstoneel" which during the 1920s helped to promote the Flemish sense of identity. In Wallonia and Brussels, the theatre is thriving and the lustre of this remarkable success is added to by the writing of some of our major writers (Michel de Ghelderode, Suzanne Lilar, Paul Willems, Henry Bauchau, Jean-Marie Piemme) and the increasing number of top quality companies (Varia, "Théâtre national" in Brussels, "Théâtre de la Place" in Liège and Plan K with its activities to promote experimental theatre for young actors). Theatre companies from the French-speaking community have performed throughout the world and acquired much recognition for the standard of their work. Because of the decentralisation going on in the two communities, this flourishing activity can be discovered throughout the country (regional dramatic art centres in the French-language community).

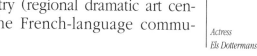

Actress
Els Dottermans

It is no accident that theatre companies should abound in the French-speaking community, for this is a reflection of a tradition which has marked this country's culture ever since the last century and is evident too in the importance assumed by lyric drama. A nation of culture, Belgium when coming into being established a link between its act of independence and the opera house. Legend has it that the 1830 Revolution began at the "Théâtre de la Monnaie", hence the desire to make the performing arts more popular.

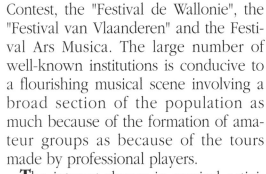

*Dancer
Michèle-Anne Demey*

A mythical image, the episode has left its mark on people's minds. The opera in Belgium continues to be one of the key ingredients of the cultural scene. The "Théâtre de la Monnaie" has become one of the chief cultural venues and its dynamism has been echoed by both the "Opéra royal de Wallonie" (Liège) and the "Opera voor Vlaanderen" (Antwerp and Ghent). Acting as a synthesis of the arts, opera is considered here as offering an overview of the cultural forms that help to make Belgium what it is. Its triumph is not simply the result of a well-turned-out and aesthetically pleasing performance. Much more than this, it bears witness to a genuine social impact. The opera house now has the opportunity to reach a wider audience, as is underscored by the reputation of the Monnaie's erstwhile director, Gérard Mortier, who now works in Salzburg, or of one its finest representatives, José Van Dam, who became the Maître de Musique in the film by Alain Corbiau.

Musical creativity is also undergoing a huge expansion and is being helped along in this by the large number of institutions (Orchestre National, Société Philharmonique, Orchestre Philharmonique de Liège, Orchestre de Chambre de Wallonie, Jeunesses Musicales, Koninklijk Filharmonisch Orkest van Vlaanderen) and the country's reputation for staging major musical events such as the International Queen Elisabeth Contest, the "Festival de Wallonie", the "Festival van Vlaanderen" and the Festival Ars Musica. The large number of well-known institutions is conducive to a flourishing musical scene involving a broad section of the population as much because of the formation of amateur groups as because of the tours made by professional players.

The interest shown in musical activities has helped to win international recognition for Belgian composers whether they be involved in contemporary music (Henri Pousseur, Frederik Van Rossum, Karel Goeyvaert, Frédéric Devreese, Bernard Foccroulle, Piet Swerts, Léo Küpper), jazz (Toots Thielemans, Steve Houben), light music (Jacques Brel, Philippe Lafontaine, Pierre Rapsat, Jo Lemaire, Maurane, Viktor Lazlo, Vaya Con Dios) or rock (The Scabs, The Kids, TC Matic, Front 242).

When it comes to the world of dance, Belgium's reputation is rooted in the work of Maurice Béjart and his Ballet of the 20th Century. His school of dancing (Mudra) has been the starting point for so many careers that Belgium is still a force to be reckoned with when it comes to choreography. In addition to the thriving folk dancing scene, modern dancing is going from strength to strength both in Flanders and Wallonia. One or two dance companies are in demand in countries that lie well beyond the Belgian borders: Micha Van Hoecke and L'Ensemble of Tournai, Anne Teresa de Keersmaeker and her group Rosas; alongside them numerous others are poised to make their mark, such as Wim Vandekeybus, Nicole Mossoux, Michèle-Anne Demey, Patricia Kuypers and José Besprosvany. Furthermore, one or two venues have come to the fore as centres of influence for Belgian choreography (Plan K in Brussels, De Singel in Antwerp) The new direction taken by the former "Ballet royal de Wallonie" (Centre chorégraphique de Charleroi) is in line with this rapidly changing landscape.

The concert Hall designed by Victor Horta in the Paleis voor Schone Kunsten during the finals of the Queen Elisabeth Music Contest

*Film maker Jaco
Van Doormael*

The Belgian cinema is going from strength to strength, which cannot be said of the film industries in most European countries. The network of activities built up in Flanders is enhancing this region's cultural identity, while at the same time casting a critical eye on Flemish society (Harry Kümel, Stijn Coninx and Urbanus). The cinema in the French-speaking community has found a niche for itself and is quite distinct from the French industry (André Delvaux, Chantal Ackerman, Marion Hänsel, Gérard Corbiau, Jaco Van Doormael). The cinema seems to be taking off in a real way in Belgium, helped along by a big improvement in the way the production and distribution channels are organised. The steps being taken in this realm by the public authorities appear to be welcomed by those involved in the industry.

An image of its time, the cinema experiences and keeps track of the present to provide us with a reflection of our uncertainties. In contrast to the cinema's role as a witness, the architect discovers his mission in taking voluntary initiatives and even in deliberately trying to have an impact on the future. In Belgium, as elsewhere, the architectural debate goes hand in hand with town planning issues. The reconstruction work combined with the social problems that had to be tackled in the post-war epoch made this planning a particularly sensitive area for political action. Some thought architecture should reflect moral values, while others wanted it to be a medium for social change (Van Kuyck, Braem). In between what were imagined to be the years of plenty in the golden sixties and the economic crisis in the seventies, the changes proved to be in many instances painful ones. The organised destruction of the country's architectural heritage stemmed from a town planning philosophy based on the judicious deployment of asphalt and bitumen. People were moving away from town centres and because of the economic recession large-scale projects were completely out of the question. With the arrival of the 1980s, architecture was re-established as an art of invention open to the imaginative paths taken by its forms (André Jacqmain, Claude Strebelle, Charles Vandenhove). Stripped of its value as a political or social project, this discipline was free to absorb tradition and take a cue from the comic strip, to take one example, so as to open up a dream-like space for citizens going about their daily tasks (Luc Schuiten) and intentionally lapse into artistic creativity (Luc Deleu).

Culture holds up a mirror to the changes in society and bears witness to its aspirations. Posters, advertising, comic strips, illustrations, graphics, design, gastronomy, interior design or fashion - they all play a key role in the social realm and make a mark on the diurnal round with their aesthetic values. There is a sense of some need to produce an effect on space in keeping with the way it is experienced by people in their daily lives. Rather than being gratuitous, this interest is connected to a tradition that ever since Art Nouveau and Art Déco has discovered some of its finest treasures turning up in Belgium. Our regions are well known for an art of living that can trace its roots back to ancestral traditions.

Artistic creativity is based on a never-ending process of transgressing our territorial borders; however, individuals are discovering that their roots are in the old traditions still alive today. The internationalisation of creative activity is set off by the permanence of a collective memory, as is testified by folklore, the art of good living and local craft activities. These traditions bespeak joy and a need to be part of a community.

The festive spirit is taken over by an art of good living which has become one of the most prized in the whole of Europe. Belgian regional products (cheeses, beer, and specialities ranging from the cramique from Brussels, to the mastelles from Ypres, via the tarte al djote from Nivelles or the baisers from Malmédy) accompany a festive spirit that would not have been disowned by Breughel himself. These festivities and recipes are centuries-old and a testimony to a world of legend preserved in the memory

*Planting the
May Tree in Brussels*

of the people from the assaults of the present. The merrymaking at carnival time in what used to be an anticipation of Lenten abstinence offers one of the privileged opportunities to discover the real Belgium. Whether it be in Binche, Eupen or Malmédy, the festivities are in full swing and provide an occasion to discover the famous Gilles of Binche, the Blanc Moussis of Stavelot or the Haguètes of Malmédy. There are numerous customs used in Belgium for reviving old traditions: the Meiboom or May Tree which announces nature's renewal in springtime; processions on the occasion of religious festivals (the Holy Blood procession in Bruges), processions which bring out the giants dating back to the 15th century (Dendermonde, Ath, Geraardsbergen, Lier and Nivelles) and the Ommegang in Brussels that takes the form of a huge spectacle reviving the ceremonies organised in 1549 in honour of Charles the Fifth and his sister Eleonore.

This symbolic universe revives a pagan pantheon built up out of legends and myths. An expression of this is to be found in the puppet theatre, which emerges in the 19th century in Liège with the famous Tchantchès and in Brussels with the Toone Theatre where the spectator is kept amused with the adventures of the hero Woltje retold in the Brussels dialect and a classical repertoire ranging from Tijl Uilenspiegel to Michel de Ghelderode, via Shakespeare or Bizet. The Puppet theatre, just like the popular theatre, preserves and performs in the living regional dialects of Flanders, Wallonia, and the German-language and Luxembourg parts of the country.

The Belgians have a strong attachment to their traditions and project upon the vestiges of their past a sentiment which lends some meaning to what has been inherited. Whether standing in front of the canals in Bruges, under the ramparts of the Gravensteen in Ghent, on the Grand-Place (main square) in Brussels or under the Perron in Liège, these testaments to the past are the symbols of an art of good living that is found in the cooking (with mussels and chips being the most obvious example), and in the traditional-style specialities kept going by establishments of high standing. A souvenir of the scale of the towns and a testament to a state of mind, the quality of life has had a large influence on the Belgian identity.

This image of Belgium served as a foundation for building up quality industries. Leatherwork with Delvaux, the flourishing haute couture industry in Antwerp, jewellery and textiles, the traditional form of creative activity in our regions is now recognised worldwide as synonymous with quality. Cooking plays a key role at this level in Belgium, touching as it does upon the philosophy of daily life as well as bordering on the purest form of artistic creativity. Whether it has a fondness for traditional cuisine or a free interpretation of the nouvelle cuisine, Belgian gastronomy establishes its pedigree at Wijnants' in Brussels as it does at Roger Souvereyns' in Limburg. Following in the wake of these artists who are concerned with producing a top quality product, just as the painter is concerned with the effects of his palette, the visual pleasure and the accuracy of his brushstrokes, an impressive number of restaurants are able to offer a style of cuisine which remains without a shadow of a doubt one of the country's best ambassadors.

By way of conclusion, it might be fitting to put this still-vibrant heritage into some sort of perspective. As a creative activity, cultural life succeeds in replying to the questions of the age and is characterised by a change in public consciousness leading the country to new structures. Caught between a rich past and an uncertain future, Belgian culture is marking out the paths, aspiring to continuity as well as reflecting upon an identity now being called into question. The cultural challenge is beginning to take the form of an escape from the Belgian condition - that "belgitude" - and exploring the special characteristics leading inevitably back to the past. Querying the language, whether it be Dutch or French, will result in a perspective in which the artist will come to grips with his past and traditions. Is it possible to imagine that the Belgian condition, which has proved to be such a stirring experience to so many, will become stabilised when Belgium, with the active cooperation of the communities, has succeeded in re-establishing a state of balance? Perhaps when history brings the two neighbouring populations with their shared memories closer together, rather than dividing them, or when the differences are used as grounds for achieving harmony rather than dissent. It might well happen, that is, unless the Belgian character succumbs to the supreme romantic irony of being able to express itself only through self-derision.

As for the question of what remains of this fine heritage and how individuals are experiencing it at the end of this 20th century, it seems that this culture lives on above all in the not insignificant form of the "art de vivre" for which it is famed all over the world. Next in the visual forms inherited from the past (architecture, painting, sculpture, illumination, jewelry/goldsmith's trade, engraving) and rooted in a landscape full of contrasts. The North sea coast with its grey luminosity still retains not only a souvenir of its fin de siècle-

charm but also the effects of painters who succeeded in depicting its
nuances (Louis Artan, Léon Spilliaert, James Ensor). It is one of the
strong points of the collective
memory of the people living within
the shelter of the 60 km of dunes
now being threatened by concrete construc-
tions and land speculation. The North Sea lent
a nice bit of colour to the dreams of children.
Located at the other end of the country the Ardennes provide a completely different landscape made up of forests, valleys waterways
and cliffs. This is a region with a different culture, another style of cooking and other types
of odours. The pleasures of the sea form a
striking contrast to the forest paths and the
sharp straight lines of the coast are rivalled by
the graduated shadings to be found in the
south of the country. In between these two regions, Belgium offers a varied selection of tones
ranging from the industrial landscapes and
built-up areas of the Borinage, to the charms of
the Flemish countryside with its low-lying farms
crushed beneath a leaden sky. The waterways
themselves are a reflection of the different cultures: the Meuse runs a tortuous path from Di-
nant to Liège, via Namur; in the countryside
near Bruges, the canals cut straight across a

peaceful country; the Semois, en-
closed in a deep valley, carries
along in its suite long wild grasses.
Each site has its own natural features, with each feature referring
to different worlds

Belœil Castle

The nation's heritage is seen
everywhere to enrich the natural resources in
the glow of its memory, as is borne out by the
Roman churches in the regions of Tournai and
Liège, the Gothic cathedrals of Mechelen, Brussels, or Antwerp, the town halls of Leuven,
Ypres, Bruges, Ghent or Brussels, the Renaissance palaces of Antwerp or Liège, the baroque
basilicas and abbeys Scherpenheuvel, Grimber-
gen or Ninove, the neo-classic complexes in
Brussels, Orval or Gembloux and the Art Nouveau houses that earned Brussels the reputation
of being the capital of this style. Not only do
these edifices have a value in themselves, they
also form part of a landscape they help to en-
hance by revealing its essence.

Midway between art and tradition, forms of
creativity have developed bearing witness to a
local culture and revealing its special features.
Lacework belongs to the Flemish landscape and
the Beguinage alike. In Brussels, Bruges, Mechelen and Antwerp it keeps alive the traditions
born of the Renaissance.

Glass and pottery-making took on a new lease of life in the wake of the Art Nouveau movement which set the industry of Wallonia aglow. In Andenne, Bouffioux (near Charleroi), Nimy (near Mons), Liège and Namur, a ceramic industry manufacturing top quality products became established. The tradition is still alive and Belgium can now boast some of the most celebrated ceramists (Lampecco, Marc Feuilien). The glass-making industry has been carried on in Hainaut since the 2nd century AD and from the 15th century onwards has been gradually making its mark by absorbing influences from Venice, England and Bohemia. Early in the last century, the crystalware made by Vonàêche (near Beauraing) held sway in the glass-making industry, but after 1826 it was superseded by the industry in Val-Saint-Lambert (near Liège) whose name is now well-known throughout the globe.

Located at the heart of the European community of the regions, at the very centre of the web of communications linking the modern major nations, Belgium has come to the fore as a land of culture and tradition. Combining a respect for the past with a joy in exploiting the vagaries of the imagination, this land has drawn attention to itself by its rich inventiveness. Eschewing avant-garde dogmas and unproductive pronouncements, it has based its cultural life on a respect for variety. Each artist has drawn up from the past a world of forms and legends continually coming to life again to interrogate the character of this "Belgian territory" and of an identity now raised to the status of a myth. At the intersection of paths spreading across the whole of Europe, Belgium has time and time again offered in various forms a very personal vision of the modern world's achievements. The future is set to reinforce its role as a focal point, in the light of the European destiny of a country that has become a federation of independent and autonomous regions. Unity bids fair to restore harmony among the communities making up this nation so that the image of a tolerant and freedom-loving people may travel well beyond its borders.

That Belgium has a future, its past never ceases to testify.

Val St. Lambert

Koen Matthijs
is Doctor of Sociology and
works at the Department for
sociology of Family, Population and Health care of
the Department of Socio-
logy at the Royal University
of Leuven. Besides diverse
articles, he has already published his studies *Suicide
and Suicide attempts,
Remarriage in Belgium,
Belgoscopy* and *Statistical
Pocket-book of Belgium.*

Michel Draguet
is Doctor of Archaeology
and History of Art (ULB).
He teaches History of Art at
the ULB. He has published
several articles on symbolism, impressionism and
avant-garde art. From 1990
till 1992, he was responsible
for Plastic Arts and Preser-
vation of Monuments and
Historical Buildings for the
cabinet of the Prime Minister
of the French-speaking
Community of Belgium.